An Insider's Guide

Get to know the
Algarve

Len Port

VIP

Vista Ibérica Publicações

3

Edition	First published in '1993
Copyright	Text : ©Len Port (1993) Paintings and drawings :©Erica Macfadyen (1993) Photographs : © Len Port and Joan Gay (1993)
Publisher	Published by Vista Ibérica Publicações, Len Port (Editorial), Peter Daughtrey (Design and Production). No. Contribuinte 900398086 28 Largo 5 de Outubro, 8400 Lagoa, Algarve.
Printer	Printed by SOCTIP - Sociedade Tipográfica, S.A. Urb. da Portela de Sacavém, 2685 Sacavém .
Thanks	Special thanks to Joan Gay and Erica Macfadyen for their special contributions. Many thanks to Nancy Denty, Brendan Ryan, Nina Christensen-Popken and Carole Golder for their help in checking the text, to Mary Burt for word processing assistance and to 'Chip' Howlett for setting the pages.

Every reasonable care has been taken by the author and publishers in presenting the information in this book, but no responsibility can be taken by them for any inaccuracies.

ISBN: 972-8044-01-1

It is the intention of the author and publishers to bring out a revised edition annually. All suggestions about up-dating the information in this edition will be gratefully received.

Map An *Insider's Tourist Map of the Algarve* is published separately by VIP as a companion to this guide.

Collaborators

Two people with special insight and long experience of the Algarve have made major contributions to this book:

Joan Gay took many of the photographs and was an invaluable mine of information and help throughout the research and writing.

Erica Macfadyen is the artist responsible for all of the line drawings and paintings, including the cover, reproduced here for the first time.

The pace of life in Portugal.

5

Contents

Welcome to "Paradise":

The Algarve at a glance

An awful lot of waffle has been written about the Algarve. There has been a tendency over the years to exaggerate. According to Artemidorus, a Greek from Ephesus who voyaged as far as the Algarve's west coast in 104BC, it was here that the gods came to rest in the evening after their labours of the day. The sun looked a hundred times bigger than anywhere else and you could hear it being extinguished as it sank into the waves. Ancient writers went on to instil terror in the hearts of Roman seafarers by pointing out that not only did the day end here - so did the world. Beyond Promontorium Sacrum, the ancient name for Cape St Vincent , you did not simply fall off the edge; you fell into an abyss seething with serpents and monsters.

Things had radically improved, however, by the Middle Ages. The Algarve was like a magnificent oasis to visiting Arabs from North Africa. They referred to it charmingly as "Sunset Land" and stayed for 500 years. At the start of the 19th century, the Algarve's reputation soared. The English poet and man of letters Robert Southey rhapsodized about the place. He called it "the Paradise of Algarve." This theme was avidly rekindled more than 150 years later with the advent of charter flights. Promotional blurb trumpeted "The Traveller's Paradise" and waxed breathlessly about this being "the stuff that dreams are made of." Once "Europe's best kept secret" was out of the bag it was not long before the developers and property salesmen were offering "a lifetime of holidays and a freehold share of Paradise." Adjectives like "luxury," "prestigious," "exquisite" and "super-luxury" were insufficient to describe their wares. Then the bubble burst. The publicity people ran out of superlatives and into difficulties in sustaining the notion of Utopia because the British press and television were on to shock-horror stories about this little corner of Heaven. The *Sunday Times* led the hue and cry in 1983 about "death in the Algarve sun" after holidaymakers suffered carbon

monoxide poisoning because of "fatal flaws" and "killer plastic." No sooner had the dust settled on that uproar than television programmes and tabloid newspapers started showing pictures of cranes and bulldozers at popular beach resorts, and protested because Paradise had become "a building site." Added to that, well aired complaints about airport congestion, pot-holed roads, unannounced water cuts, noisy motor-bikes, timeshare touts and stray dogs made a holiday in Paradise sound more like a fortnight in Purgatory. The regional tourist board did its best to countered these criticisms and it came up with a campaign slogan which proclaimed: "The Algarve is Quality." Unfortunately, the truth is a bit more long-winded than that. One thing that can be said without much contradiction, however, is that the Algarve has changed a lot. It has changed in some ways for the better, in some ways for the worse. Now that we are well into the Nineties with further change in prospect because of the EC Single Market, it is perhaps timely to review what's what, focusing mostly on facts and taking care neither to spangle the subject with star-dust nor douse it in doom and gloom. First, the fundamentals.

*T*he Algarve is a distinct geographical region and an old political province occupying the extreme south-west of continental Europe. It is roughly 155 km (95 miles) long by 50 km (30 miles) deep and is shaped

Geography

The Algarve.

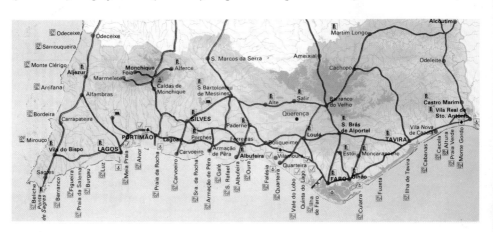

The sub-tropical climate favours vegetation which thrives on plenty of sunshine, but does not need a lot of water.

Page opposite: changing scenes and seasons.

Barlavento coast near Burgau.

like a huge amphitheatre facing south. It has an area of some 5,000 sq km (2,000 square miles), about one seventeenth of Portugal's total. In the south and west it is bounded by the Atlantic Ocean. Low mountain ranges separate it from the rest of Portugal to the north. The Guadiana River forms the frontier with the Spanish province of Andalusia in the east. So it is a compact area of modest dimensions which may be explored fairly extensively in the course of a two-week stay. Then again, you can live here for decades and still only scratch the surface.

Warm ocean currents and winds create an almost tropical climate comparable to that of North Africa or California. It is an equable climate with more than 3,000 hours of sunshine a year. The summer is dry and hot but light breezes generally prevent the heat from becoming oppressive. Spring and autumn are pleasantly mild but a light pullover will be needed in the evenings. Winter days are usually mild and often sunny, but the evenings are chilly and call for a heavy jumper or overcoat outdoors and some form of heating indoors. The annual rainfall is low compared with north-west Europe and most of it comes in the colder months. While rain is rare between June and September, wet weather lasting a week or more is not exceptional anytime between November and April.

The 125 national road, which runs the length of the Algarve from Vila Real de Santo António in the east to Vila do Bispo in the west, divides the province into two unequal and dissimilar parts. Alongside and to the south of this main highway lies the coastal strip where most of the population of 300,000 is concentrated and where tourism and associated services are the most important commercial activities. The eastern half of the coastal strip, known as the Sotavento (the leeward), comprises long sandy strands, lagoons and elongated low-lying islands. The coastline of the western half, the Barlavento (windward), is more varied: fantastically-eroded, ochre cliffs are interspersed with sweeping bays or form the backdrop to sandy coves. At Sagres, Cape St Vincent and along the west coast, the cliffs are much more formidable, rising to over 60m (200 feet).

The beaches of fine, golden sand are exposed to the open Atlantic. The rugged and often windswept west coast is sparsely populated and little developed. The intention is to keep it that way for it is an environmentally protected zone under Portuguese law.

North of the N125 national road, arable land rises through foothills to low ranges heavily forested with pine and eucalyptus. In the west, the Serra de Espinhaço de Cão joins with the Serra de Monchique, the highest point of which is Fóia at just over 900 m (3,000 feet). Moving east, there are the schistous, less habitated Serra do Caldeirão and Serra do Malhão ranges. From these mountains flow a few rivers: the Odeceixe, Oudelouca, Arade and Gilhão. The Guadiana, the Algarve's largest river, rises in Spain and flows for more that 800 km (500 miles) to enter the sea between Vila Real do Santo António and the Andalusian town of Ayamonte.

Fishing

*T*he relatively warm and shallow waters on the Continental Shelf around southern Portugal teem with both Atlantic and Mediterranean species of fish. The abundance of seafood is one of the traditional mainstays of the economy as well as providing recreation for sport fishermen. Game boats operating out of Vilamoura and Portimão hope to tackle tunny, marlin or swordfish, but more usually encounter mako or blue sharks. Commercial boats working in 15 to 25 fathoms catch large sea bream, red mullet and skate. Closer to shore, in 10 to 15 fathoms, there are plenty of bass, conger and moray eels. But of the 200 or so species of fish in Algarve waters, by far the most commercially important is the humble sardine or pilchard. It belongs to the herring family which together supplies 20 million tons or a third of the world's total annual yield of fish. At three years old, a female sardine is about 20 cm long and ready to lay between 50,000 and 60,000 eggs a season. The eggs are laid in the open sea and after a few days they hatch into larvae which continue to drift with the currents until they develop into free-swimming fish. After spawning, the adult sardines move to feeding grounds closer to shore.

Similar sized sardines gather in enormous, dense shoals which devour animal plankton as they migrate slowly northwards in summer, southward again in winter. They are caught either in drift nets which are hung out like curtains in the open sea, or lured by lights and encircled with purse seine nets. The total annual catch fluctuates, but Portugal's haul of between 60,000 and 100,000 tons is exceeded in Europe only by Spain. The arrival and unloading of the sardine boats each morning and afternoon is a time of intense and colourful quayside activity in the region's main fishing ports of Olhão and Portimão. A good proportion of the catch is immediately processed and canned for export. Fresh sardines are dispatched to markets and are an important element in the local diet. Sardines on toast, beloved by the British, bear little resemblance to the Portuguese formula of charcoal grilled, fresh, whole sardines charcoal served with home-made bread and a simple salad. Only when you have tasted that and washed it down with well chilled white or *verde* wine have you had a real taste of the Algarve.

Tunny or tuna fishing and canning used to be of great commercial importance in the Algarve, but no more. The tunny were caught in enormous, elaborate traps consisting of a series of net chambers fixed to the sea bed in shallow water. Once entrapped in the last chamber, the migrating tunny were gaffed from boats and hauled on board in a bloody spectacle referred as "the bullfight of the sea." In the Seventies, the tunny suddenly changed their migratory path. They began giving the Algarve a wide berth which meant that once busy canning factories were forced to close. The factories now stand derelict and crumbling.

Farming

*F*or many centuries the main crops produced in the Algarve were almonds, olives, figs, carobs and grapes. Not needing a lot of water, they thrive on inferior soils and in areas where the rainfall is lightest. Grapes are still produced in considerable quantity, but the production of almonds, olives, figs and carobs has dropped sharply due to the decline of cheap labour and other economic factors. More than half of the region's working population used to work on the land. That was before more pay, less hours and better conditions in the service and building industries prompted a shift from rural areas to the towns and the coast leaving deserted cottages and orchards to be replaced by holiday complexes, and golf courses - or in many cases not replaced at all but simply allowed to peacefully decay.

The Algarve's most characteristic tree, the almond, is not a native of this country. It is indigenous to south-west Asia and North Africa. How it came to be so plentiful here is the subject of an oft-told folk tale about a Moorish king of the Algarve and his Scandinavian princess who pined for home. To cure her affliction the king had a bright idea. He imported a load of almond trees and planted them everywhere within sight of the princess's bedroom window. When they came into blossom in what would still be winter in Scandinavia, the countryside all around the castle appeared to be covered with snowflakes. The story has a happy-ever-after ending, of course, but it could be that commoners

Spring snowflakes.

Of mules and men.

of a more mercantile nature also had something to do with the introduction of almond trees which have been cultivated since the Middle Ages, not so much to look lovely in February as to yield valuable fruit the following September. Both bitter and sweet almonds are grown commercially. When it has ripened, the fruit is knocked from the trees by men wielding long poles. Laid out to dry in the sun, the leathery hull splits open, curls outwards and discharges the inner nut which then has to be shelled. It is a laborious and time consuming business. Portugal is one of the world's leading exporters of shelled almonds which are marketed whole or used in confectionery. Processed almond oil is used as a flavouring essence and in the preparation of cosmetics and pharmaceuticals. Almond cake is an Algarve speciality.

The cork oak is a much more robust tree than the almond.

16

The evergreen olive tree blossoms much later and much less spectacularly than the almond, but the harvesting of the fruit in autumn and its subsequent processing is just as arduous. The green or black fruit is extremely bitter and remains inedible until treated to neutralize the glucoside it contains. Ripe olives also contain oil amounting to between 20% and 30% of the weight of the fruit minus the pip. Immature olives are gathered for eventual bottling and eating. It is the fully ripened fruit which is pressed to extract oil used in cooking and as a preservative for canned fish.

The fig, like the olive, was one of the earliest fruit trees to be cultivated by primitive man. Bacchus, the god of fruitfullness and vegetation, held it to be sacred, yet among the ancient Greeks it was a staple food. In most Mediterranean countries, right up to modern times, peasant communities depended heavily on figs in their diet and so it was widely known as "poor man's food." Fig consumption has waned in recent years, but two crops are harvested annually (June and August) and marketed fresh in the Algarve. Fresh figs, with their well known laxative qualities, are high in minerals such as calcium and phosphorus. Dried figs are high in iron.

The carob grows taller and with its glossy evergreen leaves offers more shade than the other traditional fruit trees in the region. The "locusts" eaten by St John in the Bible were carob pods. They look like large pea pods until they blacken and fall to the ground in August. A large, mature tree may yield as much as 450 kg of pods each year. The edible, fleshy pulp of the pods is rich in protein and contains about 50% sugar. So carobs have a commercial value when gathered and dried. They kept the Duke of Wellington's horses going in Portugal and Spain during the Peninsular War and their main use today is still for animal feed. They are also used in the making of chocolate products. The seeds contain a gum used in the textile, pharmaceutical, leather and cosmetic industries. The remarkable uniformity of their size was why carob seeds or ''carats'' were originally used to weigh gold.

Almond, olive, fig and carob orchards in many places have been abandoned or replaced, but the area

Olives (above) are eaten when black and ripe, or after being pickled while still green.
Carob pods (below) turn from green to black as they ripen in summer.

devoted to the growing of grapes is stable at about 13,500 acres mainly in the vicinities of Tavira, Lagoa and Lagos. Early ripening greenhouse grapes are ready in mid-June. Outdoor table grapes (mainly around Tavira) are harvested between mid-July and mid-October. Wine grapes, which account for about 70% of all Algarve grapes, are mostly picked in September. The job is done by local women armed with sun-hats and secateurs who ride out to the vineyards on the backs of lorries early in the morning. They snip, chat and sing their way through the day along the seemingly endless rows of vines. Bruised or over-ripe table grapes must be pruned out. Bunches are handled with care and dispatched to markets in paper-lined boxes. Working with wine grapes is easier. They are cut from the vines and tossed willy-nilly into baskets and then into open trailers and trucks bound for winery presses.

Cork is grown in the hillier areas of the Algarve but only in a small way compared with the vast plantations farther north in Portugal. It is the thick, outer bark of

Gathering grapes.

the cork oak tree which provides the raw material for bottle stoppers, processed panels and tiles. Portuguese law forbids the stripping of trees of less than a prescribed circumference usually reached when the trees are 15 years old. Thereafter, trees may be stripped only every ninth year. You will notice a number, between 0 and 9, painted on the trunk of each cork oak tree. This indicates the year it was last stripped. The stripping is done between May and mid-September when the adhesion between the inner and outer bark is at its weakest. Care is taken to avoid damaging the regenerative inner bark while sufficient outer bark is always left intact to insure continued health and growth. The first stripping yields "virgin" bark of poor quality. The second is better. The finest comes from the third and subsequent strippings. The raw, semi-circular bark is taken to factories near Silves and São Brás de Alportel where it is boiled to remove tannin, and flattened. Good quality bark ends up as bottle stoppers. The trimmings and lower quality bark is processed into tiles and sheets to be used for sound-proofing and insulation.

Cork oak bark is stripped, stacked and left to dry before being taken to the factories.

Farming methods in southern Portugal until very recently remained stubbornly ancestral and inefficient. Some fields out towards the west coast are still ploughed by oxen. In the north-east of the province, hillside fields of wheat are still sown and reaped entirely by hand. Carts pulled by donkeys and mules on their way to town markets still compete with motorized traffic. Such sights are quickly disappearing, however. The inevitable spread of mechanization and modern irrigation methods have greatly boosted citrus growing. Oranges, lemons and grapefruit need more careful cultivation and a lot more water than the traditional big five crops. Production is less labour intensive and more profitable than almonds, olives, figs, carobs and even grapes. Grown in barely commercial quantities a couple of decades or so ago, oranges are now the Algarve's number one agricultural earner. Although mainly winter ripening, oranges are all-year-round fruit here. Both tight-skinned sweet oranges and loose-skinned Mandarins are grown in quantity. Big, juicy Baias with

Early days in he annual production of wine grapes on a typical Lagoa smallholding.

their distinctive navel (picked January to May), small seedless Satsumas (picked October and November), Clementines (November and December) and Tangerines (January to April) are but a few of the varieties grown mostly for the Lisbon, Oporto and overseas markets.

You can't grow decent Brambleys or Granny Smiths in the Algarve. The weather isn't right for them. On the other hand it is perfect for apricots, avocados, loquats, peaches, nectarines, plums, pomegranates and strawberries. Vegetables, like fruit, ripen earlier in the sunny south than elsewhere in Portugal and that places a high demand on the produce of thousands of small farms, kitchen gardens and plots where the soil is reasonable and there is adequate water at hand. As virtually all of the fruit and vegetables consumed in the Algarve are fresh and locally grown, there tends to be either a glut of any one type or, out of season, none at all. It arrives in the markets and shops in all shapes and sizes, EC standardization not having taken effect here yet, but it is grown under natural rather than artificial conditions and tastes as wholesome as it really is.

Loquats (above) are ready for picking in May. Oranges (below) are picked throughout winter and spring.

Although membership of the EC has given much impetus to agriculture, some major problems remain. Portugal's farms continue to be the least productive in Europe. Over 20 per cent of Portuguese workers - more than any other EC country except Greece - work on the land, yet Portugal still has to import half the food it eats. Far higher efficiency at a much higher technical level is being strenuously promoted with EC aid. Huge sums are being provided over a current 10 year period to help expand rural roads, irrigation, electrification, technical training and a wide range of other reforms. It is all part of an overall modernization programme and a major revamping of the national economy.

Economy

*P*ortugal has long been the poorest country in Western Europe. At the turn of the century she was virtually bankrupt, a condition which did not improve with the switch from a monarchy to a republic in 1910, the outbreak of the First World War in 1914, or the domestic upheavals which continued for eight years after the 1918 armistice. The economy was only brought under control after the military dissolved parliament and suspended the constitution in 1926. The man who master-minded this was António de Oliveira Salazar, the new finance minister. Later, as prime minister, he ruled as dictator of a one party state which banned trade unions and strikes. Under Salazar's tight grip, the country experienced an unprecedented rate of growth. In the Nineteen-fifties and sixties Salazar presided over great improvements in the nation's road, rail, telephone and hydroelectric systems, and in the provision of housing for workers and education for children. The advances in industry were considerable, particularly in textiles. Agriculture, however, remained woefully backward. During the Nineteen-sixties and early seventies massive amounts of money and manpower were pumped into trying to sustain the unwinnable wars in Portugal's African empire. The revolution at home in 1974 ended this crippling drain, but it led to new economic difficulties on a huge scale. Banks and insurance companies as well as heavy and basic industries were nationalized by the newly formed

Salazar (1889 - 1971). After a spell as Minister of Finance with extraordinary powers, he was elevated to Prime Minister in 1932. His dictatorship ended when he suffered a totally disabling stroke in 1968.

or liberated left-wing groupings. Large estates were expropriated. Family-owned businesses were taken over by workers, investment dried up, productivity plummeted, unemployment soared. The highly volatile post-revolutionary period in the mid-Seventies also saw Portugal grappling with the problem of 700,000 refugees arriving from Africa. On top of all this Portugal had to contend with an international oil crisis and a world-wide recession.

Portugal's economic recovery stemmed from a tough International Monetary Fund adjustment programme in 1983/4. It was fuelled by falling oil prices and funds from the European Community of which Portugal became a full member in 1986. During its first five years of membership, Portugal's economy grew at a faster rate than any other of the Twelve. Also high, phenomenally high, was the growth in the annual rate of foreign investment - up from US$164 million in 1985 to $5.5 billion in 1991. As capitalisim consolidated with a series of smooth privatisations of major companies, the gross domestic product increased by an average of 4.3% a year. Exports were up 10% a year. Inflation dropped from 30% in the early Eighties to 9% in 1991. Unemployment was brought down to 4% of the labour force of more than 4.5 million. Low labour costs were a major attraction for foreign investors. On the other hand, low wages were the cause of much worker discontent. Average wages in 1990 were a third of those in Spain and a fifth of those in Germany. While living standards have soared, they are still low by European standards. While the economy has developed and stabilised, full integration with the EMS is not expected to be easy.

Tourism

*M*ore than in any other region of the country, tourism has become enormously important to the economy of the Algarve and it is now a far bigger earner than fishing and farming combined. As the number of visitors from abroad soared in the Eighties there was an accompanying building boom mainly along the most tourist intensive stretch of the Algarve south coast, from Faro to Alvor. Most of the funding for the mushrooming holiday complexes, individual villas and timeshare apartments came from Britain. While tourism and the closely linked property market provided many jobs and huge injections of foreign money, it also meant that the prosperity of the Algarve had become dependent to a discomforting extent on the vagaries of the British economy. With most of their eggs in one basket liable to be broken by sudden changes in British interest rates and other factors beyond their control, Algarve planners tried to dilute the British influence by wooing more ardently than ever before potential tourists and investors in other EC countries, Scandinavia, North America and the Far East. Despite this continuing effort and the opening of EC borders under the Single Market, Britons are likely to continue to account for a high proportion of the visitors, holiday home-owners and foreign residents in the Algarve. Of course, the large-scale influx of foreigners over the past 20 years has prompted some changes in the life-style of the local

Derelict fish canneries remain today as a reminder of the economic strife of the 1970s.

Ancient History

*The entrance to a
Neolithic burial chamber
at Alcalar.*

*Archaeologists
examine the
remanants of a
Roman water cistern*

inhabitants. It is not the first time this happened. The Algarve has been inundated by innovative foreigners several times before, albeit a long time ago.

*T*he roots of civilisation in southern Portugal go back to prehistoric times. The very earliest human inhabitants devoted most of their energies to hunting, fishing, collecting shellfish and gathering wild fruits, nuts and berries. Their tools were made from stone and bone. Almost everything else about the life-style of these palaeolithic people is guesswork, but it is unlikely that their primitive culture changed very much in thousands of years. By about 3000 BC, during the Neolithic Age, a much more advanced form of mankind arrived on the scene having migrated westwards along the shores of the Mediterranean. For the first time the Algarve was settled by people who tilled the soil, domesticated animals, built dwellings, made pottery and worked with copper. Stone burial chambers or dolmens were characteristic of this period. Several are preserved in the countryside of Alcalar not far from Portimão. The "Iberians," a term loosely used to mean indigenous people living in parts of south-west Europe from the Bronze Age, were described by ancient writers as small in stature, wiry with high cheekbones and dark complexions. In the 7th and 6th centuries BC they were infused and dominated by Celtic tribes from beyond the Pyrenees. The Celts, a pastoral race skilled in working with iron, dominated northern and central Portugal, but were less influential in the far south. From the far end of the Mediterranean, at about the same time as the Celts, came the Phoenicians. They set up trading stations on the Andalusian and Algarve coasts, especially at the mouths of large rivers such as the Guadalquivir and the Guadiana. The Phoenicians were mainly interested in bartering eastern goods for tin, copper and silver from the Iberian interior. They were joined or succeeded in the 6th century BC by Greek traders until the Carthaginians closed the Straits of Gibraltar to their Mediterranean rivals and assumed commercial control beyond the fabled Pillars of Hercules. So, during the first

24

millennium before Christ, successive waves of people infiltrated or invaded southern Portugal. From the north came Celts. From the east came Phoenicians followed by Greeks and then Carthaginians. But the various peoples who came and went over this long, early period left little evidence of their cultures. The same cannot be said of the next great wave from the east - the Romans.

Early in the second century before Christ, Roman legions advanced through the Iberian peninsula quelling all the tribal groups who opposed them. The Lusitanians, who lived in central Portugal, proved to be the most formidable of all the opposing native peoples. The Lusitanians fought long and fiercely well beyond the boundaries of their native land. Eventually, after the death of the greatest of all Lusitanian warriors, Viriathus, "the Hannibal of the Iberians," the Romanisation of central Portugal began. The year was 137 BC. The influence of the Romans between then and the arrival of Germanic tribes in the 5th century AD was profound throughout Portugal. They implanted their language, laws, religion and customs. They built cities and connected them with highways one of which ran from Ossonoba (Faro) to Olissipo (Lisbon). Remnants of Roman buildings and artefacts survive in the Algarve, notably at Estói not far from Faro, but the most enduring Roman legacies are those ingrained in the people.

Mosaic floors, like above, are among the many relics from centuries of Roman rule.
Below: a Visigothic oil lamp, but the Germanic invaders left few artefacts.

Middle Ages

*W*hereas the Visigoths and other barbarian invaders failed to make much of a mark on the south of Portugal, that of the Moors, who eventually swept them aside, is indelible. The Moors, Muslim Arabs and Berbers from North Africa, arrived in the 8th century. They quickly conquered the whole of Portugal, but their domination survived longest and had the greatest lasting impact in the Algarve. The Moors were here for well over 500 years. The name Algarve is derived from the Arabic *Al-Garb* meaning the land to the west. It referred to the region's geographical position within the vast Moorish empire whose caliphates, or central governments, were in Damascus, Syria, and later

Córdoba, Spain.

Portugal as an independent state was born in the 12th century when it detached itself from the neighbouring Spanish kingdom of Leon while continuing the protracted Christian reconquest southward against the Moors with the help of northern European Crusaders. The Moors were finally expelled from their last Algarve stronghold in 1253 by Afonso III. He was proclaimed ''King of Portugal and the Algarve,'' a title which reflected the Algarvean sense of separate identity which still persists in milder form today.

The *Algarvios*, like the Cornish in England for example, have always considered themselves a people apart, but since the final banishment of the Moors in the mid-13th century the Algarve has been an integral part of Portugal, its history and fortunes closely intertwined with those of the rest of the country. Portuguese sovereignty over the province was confirmed in a treaty with the more powerful kingdom of Castile in 1297; but it was Castile's belligerence towards Portugal in the following century which gave rise to a far more famous treaty - the Treaty of Windsor.

The tile panel below forms the back of a shady park bench in Portimão and depicts the Portuguese arrival in Brazil in 1500.

26

Signed by Portugal and Britain in 1386, the Treaty of Windsor still stands today. It is the basis of the fact that Portugal is Britain's oldest ally. The treaty pledges "an inviolable, eternal, strong, perpetual and true league of friendship, alliance and union" between the two countries. Portugal's friendship with Britain in the 14th century was further cemented by the marriage of King João I and Philippa of Lancaster, daughter of John of Gaunt. Their third surviving son was Henry the Navigator who spent most of his life in the Algarve laying the foundations for the world's greatest voyages of discovery. More on the Algarve's most distinguished celebrity later. Suffice here to say that his leadership was the key to Portugal relentlessly pushing back the known frontiers of the world. It opened the way for Columbus, Vasco da Gama and Magellan. Many of the epoch-making voyages of the late 15th century set sail from the western Algarve and many Algarve seamen were among the pioneers who discovered new lands, civilisations and riches in Africa, the Americas and Asia. Traders and colonisers followed in their wake. Portugal in the 16th century became a superpower with an empire out of all proportion to her tiny size. This was her "golden era," the most illustrious period in her history, in which the Algarve played a most significant part. It was in the third quarter of the 16th century that things began to go badly wrong for Portugal. The Algarve played a most significant part in that too.

King Sebastião, who was particularly fond of the Algarve, was single-handedly responsible for Portugal's downfall as a superpower. Because of him, all that was great and glorious about Portugal came to an abrupt end in the year 1578. Whether he was just young and headstrong or whether he was stark, raving mad is debatable, but at the age of 24 he sailed from the Algarve with more than 23,000 men with the fanciful idea of conducting a latter-day crusade against the Moors. What a debacle it turned out to be. At the Battle of Alcacer-Quivir in Morocco, the king and 8,000 of his followers were killed; the rest of the hopelessly outmanoeuvred Portuguese troops were taken prisoner. Sebastião's death meant that the Portuguese crown

This statue of Henry the Navigator stands in a square in Lagos from where many voyages of discovery began.

Christopher Columbus spent a lot of time in Portugal. He married a Portuguese girl and some historians argue he himself was a Portuguese.

27

Above: Portugal's adventurers abroad always took with them the symbol of Christianity. Below: Invasion sails set.
Original in Greenwich Museum

Sebastião's death meant that the Portuguese crown passed to his great-uncle Henrique, a cardinal whose celibacy and advanced years assured an ignominious end to the House of Avis, the pedigree of some of Portugal's greatest monarchs. After that, the Portuguese crown passed to a Spaniard. Surprisingly, Sebastião was still revered after his death by a nation convinced that like a messiah, he would return. Even more surprisingly, he is regarded as something of a national hero still - enough so to have streets named after him.

It was Philip II of Spain who pressed the Spanish claim to the vacant throne of Portugal by invading in 1580. Thus for Portugal began a humiliating period of 60 years under Spanish rule As a mere annex of its much larger Iberian neighbour, Portugal was dragged into Spanish wars against England, Holland and France. It was from Lisbon in 1588 that the Invincible Spanish Armada set sail to invade England. Most of the Armada warships had been built in Lisbon and many of their crew were Portuguese. It was around this time that England's Elizabeth I sent forces which attacked the

Algarve. Sir Francis Drake razed Henry the Navigator's reputed former headquarters at Sagres. The Earl of Essex sacked Faro. In the 17th century, Portugal managed to regain control of her homeland and some of her former empire, including Brazil. In the 18th century, gold and diamonds from Brazil helped finance an epoch of great pomp and splendour at home. The arts and sciences were fostered and great impetus was given to agriculture and industry. Fine buildings were constructed all over the country, but all of those in the Algarve were destroyed or severely damaged by a massive earthquake in 1755. Lisbon was also devastated by the earthquake - Europe's worst ever - which is thought to have killed up to 60,000 people, many of whom were attending Mass at the time.

There was further widespread devastation a little over half a century later as a result of three successive French invasions during the Napoleonic campaigns. The French, who had occupied the whole of Portugal in 1807, were finally expelled in 1810 by General Arthur Wellesley, later Duke of Wellington. The French Revolution was followed by a revolution in Portugal (1820), a counter-revolution (1828) and a civil war (1832 - 34), a problematic period which was merely a prelude to another one hundred years of extraordinary political, social and economic upheaval.

Vestiges of turbulent times...

V irtually every town in Portugal has a street named in commemoration of October 5. Portugal was proclaimed a republic on October 5, 1910, the monarchy having been abolished earlier that year. The Republic brought no instant cure to the country's chronic ills. On the contrary, there was an average of one coup and almost three governments a year between 1910 and 1926. Against a background of chaos, António de Oliviera Salazar, a professor of law, was asked by the military dictatorship in 1928 to take on the job of finance minister. He did a brilliant job and was elevated to prime minister in 1952. From then until his death from a stroke in 1968, Salazar was the dominant figure in an extreme right-wing, one-party state.

20th-century history

Meanwhile, Portugal had fought with the Allies during the First World War. She favoured General Franco in the Spanish Civil War but remained officially neutral. Although she took no part and was officially neutral in the Second World War, she allowed Britain use of military facilities in the Azores under the provisions of the Treaty of Windsor. In the Nineteen-sixties, Portugal became increasingly engulfed in wars of her own in her African territories of Guinea-Bissau, Angola and Mozambique. These guerrilla wars lasted 13 years and were finally brought to an end by a military coup d'etat at home.

Rua 25 de Abril is another street name found in every town and village in Portugal for it was on that date in 1974 that the most remarkable event in recent Portuguese history occurred. Units of the armed services occupied key buildings in the centre of Lisbon and overthrew the government of Salazar's successor, Marcello Caetano. The coup was led by young officers, mostly army captains, who wanted an immediate end to dictatorship, colonialism and the futile wars in Africa. They pledged parliamentary democracy, freedom of speech, the right to strike and other fundamental political and social changes in Western Europe's most repressed state. It was a hugely popular and almost bloodless coup symbolised by red carnations in the barrels of guns, but the transition from nearly half a century of right-wing totalitarianism to a stable democracy was an intensely turbulent period.

Politics

Two moderate parties, the centre-left Socialists and the centre-right Social Democrats, emerged the strongest. Under Portugal's system of proportional representation there were frequent elections and changes of government as one coalition after another collapsed. Then in the general election of 1987, the first absolute majority since the revolution, and indeed this century, was won by the Social Democrats. They repeated their victory in the general election of 1991 thus extending for another four years the political stability the country had long needed. An important factor in sustaining that stability was the harmonious working relationship between the Social Democrat Prime Minister, Anibal Cavaco Silva, and the veteran Socialist leader and elected head of state, Mário Soares. Cavaco Silva is from the Algarve. His erstwhile political foe, Soares, has had a home here for many years. Both are currently serving second terms in office.

Portugal's President is elected for five years. He holds no executive powers and does not involve himself with either the day-to-day running of the country or party politics, but because of the personal influence he is able to exert his position is rather more than merely that of a figurehead. Mário Soares, who founded the Portuguese Socialist Party while in exile in Germany, returned to Portugal after the April 25 revolution to become the country's most distinguished leader. He succeeded General António Ramalho Eanes in 1986 as Portugal's first civilian head of state in six decades.

The right-wing CDS, Christian Democratic Party, is one of the less successful of Portugal's main political groups.

The 254 members of Portugal's parliament, the Assemblia de República, are also elected for five years. Their constituencies are called administrative districts and the administrative district of Faro corresponds with the historical province of the Algarve. Each district is divided into municipal councils or *câmaras* of which the Algarve has 16. Local elections are held every five years with most of the candidates aligned to one or other of the national political parties.

*I*t is not possible to be so precise about the cosmopolitan population of the Algarve, but of the 10 million people in Portugal about 300,000 live in the southern province. This includes the majority indigenous Algarveans or *Algarvios,* as well as workers from more northern parts of the country, immigrants from former colonies, and foreign nationals from Britain, Germany, Holland, Scandinavia, the United States and a host of other countries. The fact that the Algarve is so cosmopolitan is an indication of the natural hospitality of the Algarveans.

It is said that the Moors are responsible for the Algarvean innate sense of heritage, nonchalant acceptance of the present and fatalistic view of the future. This, perhaps, helps explains the trait which

People and life-styles

most confounds visitors from northern Europe: the Algarvean attitude towards time. The people of southern Portugal have a wonderfully under-developed sense of urgency about almost everything. They refuse to rush. The English proverb about not putting off until tomorrow what you can do today does not apply. It could be roughly translated in the Algarve to mean why do today what you can put off until tomorrow - or next week? Punctuality is a totally alien concept. Foreigners tend to become frustrated, if not infuriated, when things do not happen on time and according to plan, but Algarveans maintain their normal blood pressure, shrug their shoulders and sum up life's minor setbacks with one of their favourite expressions: *não faz mal* - "never mind." *De nada* - "it's nothing" - is another common expression. It is used in response to thanks for any help or kindness however great.

People in the Algarve are formally polite with their handshakes and kisses to both cheeks and their *bom dia*, *boa tarde* and *boa noite* greetings, but other than that they do not stand much on ceremony. For example, suits and ties are not out of place in the evening in top hotels and restaurants, but the normal mode of dress almost everywhere is informal. Some tourists take this to extremes by walking around town centres and into shops and banks dressed only in shorts or beach-wear. Locals regard this as crass. Also frowned upon is rude, rowdy or drunken behaviour in public, because Algarveans in general are courteous, conservative and mild-mannered.

Compared with their Spanish neighbours in Andalusia, the Portuguese are soft-spoken though that does not mean they are not extremely talkative. Like most southern Europeans, they are great conversationalists. Portuguese, the world's seventh most widely spoken language, is the mother tongue of about 130 million people. When written, it resembles Spanish but in pronunciation it is very different. Although they are related, they are quite separate languages. English is now the main second language taught in Portuguese schools. Portuguese who deal with tourists often understand English well, but they are in the minority. English is spoken by hotel receptionists and airline staff, for example, by many waiters and some shop assistants, but by few taxi drivers, policemen, maids or mechanics. Although few Portuguese speak English or any other foreign language, and fewer foreigners speak Portuguese, this is rarely a problem that cannot be overcome by sign language and perhaps a few key words and phrases if you cannot find an obliging interpreter.

Wine

Cafes in their many forms are where local gossip is exchanged, topical matters ardently discussed and business deals negotiated over coffee, usually small cups of black *expresso* coffee called *bicas* , often complemented by a glass or two of brandy. The liquor licensing laws are very liberal and all types of alcoholic drinks are served in restaurants, street cafes, pubs and beach bars, rural *tabernas* and *tascas,* even in cake shops. By volume, the most popular beverage is chilled

lager beer. Next to brandy, Scotch whisky is the preferred spirit. Farmers and fishermen enjoy a regional firewater called *medronho* which is a clear aguardiente made from *arbutus* berries which grow wild on the hillsides. Inevitably there is a fig aguardiente *(figo),* an almond-based liqueur *(amêndoa amarga)* and a sweet and strong combination of brandy and locally-produced honey called *brandy-mel.*

Portugal is, of course, a wine country and its wines run the gamut from prickly *vinho verdes* through immensely popular *rosés* and fruity whites to robust reds and venerable ports. Wines to suit every palate and pocket are on sale in all restaurants and supermarkets. *Verde* (green) wines are so named because of their youth. Sometimes red, more commonly white, they are bottled when only four or five months old. They are very light, tartish and slightly bubbly; a refreshing summertime drink when well chilled, and an ideal companion to seafood or chicken dishes. *Vinho verde* is produced in the north-west of Portugal from grapes grown on small, intensively cultivated plots by about 55,000 farmers. This, the most densely populated part of the country, is also where Portugal's best champagne-style wine comes from. It does not match its French counterpart in prestige, but its remarkably low price is reason enough for a celebration. From the other end of the country also comes the best of Portugal's famous pink wines, hundreds of thousands of cases of which are exported each year to the United States and the United Kingdom. The international popularity of Mateus Rosé in particular is nothing short of phenomenal.

Like the *verde,* champagne-style and *rosé* wines, the best whites and reds are grown and produced under strict control in legally marked-out areas. They carry a seal of origin to ensure quality. One of the best known of the demarcated areas is the wild and mountainous Dão region which has been producing fine table wines for at least seven centuries. It lies within the triangle formed by the cities of Viseu, Guarda and Coimbra in north-central Portugal. In contrast to the harshness of the Dão countryside and the rudimentary life-style of its people, the chief characteristics of Dão wines are their smoothness and suavity. Planting often involves blasting through granite on terraced hillsides, but at the other end of the production line flows fresh, light-coloured whites and far greater quantities of full-bodied, velvety reds. The much smaller Bucelas wine-growing area just north of Lisbon is sheltered by a ring of mountains. They harbour a mild mico-climate reflected in the white wines which are very light with a delicate bouquet; the reds with age take on the colour of topaz. To the west, the vines of one of Europe's most unusual demarcated areas, Colares, are grown on shifting sand dunes next to the Atlantic Ocean. Because of the great depth to which the roots must go to reach firm soil, the vines of Colares were not affected by the scourge of Phylloxera, the pest which devastated continental vineyards towards the end of the last century. Like the dunes, colares wines are generally very smooth. Earlier last century, during the Peninsular War, the wines of the Carcavalos area outside of Lisbon got rave reviews from the Duke of Wellington's officers. Full-bodied and fortified with local brandy, these wines have an alcoholic strength of 19% compared with the 11.5% to 12.5% which is the norm among

Vinho verde wines go well with fish dishes.

unfortified table wines. No wonder Wellington's men fought bravely. They might have had marginally less courage had they drunk the golden, dessert wines from the Setúbal area south of Lisbon where the Muscatel is normally 18%. Port, the most famous of all Portuguese wines, is commonly 20%.

There is Californian port, Australian port, South African port and even British port, but there is only one Port with a capital P and it comes from the Upper Douro region of northern Portugal, the first wine-growing region in the world to be officially demarcated. The Marquis of Pombal had the foresight to do this in 1756. The land marked out then and since expanded extends along the rugged, precipitous flanks of the Douro river valley to the Spanish border. The terraced vineyards on beds of schist and granite are lashed by storms during the bitterly cold winter months and parched during the searing hot summers. Originally they produced only rough red much of which was imported by Portugal's close seafaring ally, Britain, but it did not travel well. To help it travel and probably to enhance its general appeal in 18th century England, they developed the process of adding brandy to arrest the fermentation so that the wine retained some of its natural sweetness. British merchants played a leading role in the refinement of this process and the development of the wines of the Upper Douro to their unparalleled level of excellence. From the early 18th century to the end of the 19th, more Port than any other type of wine was consumed in England. It was not until the 19th century that other countries began importing it in any large quantities. English family names are deeply rooted and are still closely involved in the Port trade, but it is the French who drink more of it than anyone else nowadays. The Scandinavians drink the most per capita. Only 8% of the total annual output is consumed within Portugal itself.

The Algarve consumes all the wine it produces and a lot more besides. It produces a little port wine, but it is port with a small p. The vast bulk of the province's considerable output is ordinary table wine, mainly red, which is not held in much esteem by the connoisseurs.

It has no pretensions to be other than reasonably palatable plonk. It comes from wine-growers' co-operatives and a few small, private *adegas* in one and five litre bottles stocked by all supermarkets along with selections of better quality wines from farther north. The chief features of Algarve wine taken as a whole are its high alcoholic content and low price - potentially a heady mix. For reasons to do with basic economics as much as snobbery, Algarve wines are seldom stocked by local restaurants even though all restaurants are required by law to offer inexpensive house wine in addition to any better labels they may carry.

Grapes on their way to the winery.

Food

*B*y international standards there are a few excellent and some very good restaurants in the Algarve. What the vast number of more ordinary establishments lack in sophistication of cuisine, service and decor they compensate for with honest-to-goodness cooking and uncomplicated conviviality. Down-to-earth wholesomeness is rated higher than fancy embellishments. Junk food has yet to establish a serious foothold in a corner of Europe where natural freshness still takes precedence over appearances and packaging. The more adventurous visitors who scrutinize Algarve menus will want to look beyond the internationally familiar meat and vegetable dishes and try *amêijoas na cataplana* (clams, spiced sausage, cured ham, onions and garlic steamed together); *caldeirada de peixe* (various types of fish and shellfish stewed in their own juices with onions, tomatoes and peppers) ; *bacalhau à brás* (dried salted cod fried with potatoes, onions, garlic and scrambled egg); or *lulas recheadas* (squid stuffed with bacon, spiced sausage, rice, tomato and onion cooked in a white wine sauce). And somewhere between the *caldo verde* (cabbage soup) and the *morgado de amêndoa* (fruit shaped marzipan) or the *touchino do céu* (almond egg cake dessert) you may be able to soak up a little bit of Portuguese culture. Restaurants serving typical Algarvean dishes sometimes feature *fado*.

Cooking over charcoal embers is traditional and still popular. On cottage doorsteps and restaurant forecourts you'll come across the summer sound and smell of sizzling barbecues.

Music

*R*oughly speaking, *fado* is to Portugal what flamenco is to Spain. Its origins are misty, but it seems to have started out as lewd entertainment much enjoyed by African slaves. It developed into music of the bars and brothels frequented by Portuguese seamen. It remained risque but became increasingly popular and attracted wider audiences in the second half of the last century. It has since been cleaned up and elevated to high respectability, so much so that it has come to be regarded as an expression of the soul of the nation. It is difficult to grasp the depth of emotions and patriotic fervour it evokes. Essentially ballad folk music, it is sung with great passion by a single male or female vocalist, a *fadista,* accompanied by two or more musicians playing guitar-like instruments. There is a lofty formality about the agonised melodies and forlorn lyrics of the Coimbra strain of *fado* which bemoans forlorn hopes, lost loves and wrecked lives. Even the most popular sing-a-long tunes of the jollier Lisbon form of *fado* are delivered with a measured stiffness that keeps Portuguese audiences spellbound. The first few bars of a *fado* favourite are enough to transport middle-aged fans into raptures. Uncomprehending foreigners may even find themselves moved by the intensity of all this indulgence in bittersweet sadness, a condition on the darker side of nostalgia the Portuguese call *saudades.*

Fadistas.

Fado's country counterpart is altogether less emotive. Straight- forward rhythms played on a couple of guitars, an accordion, a fiddle and a drum lay down a lively sound for round dancing at festivals and rural get-togethers called *bailes* which are attended with equal enthusiasm by all the family, young and old. This sort of music is generally only heard live on special occasions, but some radio stations give it plenty of air time. Recorded pop music is as ubiquitous in southern Portugal as anywhere else, and there is a surprisingly widespread interest in modern jazz. Many of the bands playing in bars have strong African or Brazilian influences. At the other end of the musical spectrum, an annual spring music festival spread over several months, venues and towns features a wide range of concert performances by visiting classical musicians.

The arts

In the fine arts as in music, the Algarve cannot pretend to be a cultural oasis but nor is it a desert. Southern Portugal has a clarity of light, a brilliance of colour and an array of distinctive subject matters which inspire painters and photographers. Ocean breezes are perpetually clearing the Algarve air which is virtually pollution-free anyway because of low traffic densities and the absence of industrial gaseous wastes. Crystal clear air together with bright sunshine, low horizons and an almost 360 degree vault of often cloudless sky allow unusual sharpness of vision. The colours of the coast and countryside are mainly vivid blues, pale ochres and lush greens splashed with sensational magenta sunsets. The natural beauty of landscapes and seascapes together with the picturesque simplicity of traditional life-styles have attracted a growing number of professional artists and photographers in recent years, and more and more commercial art galleries have opened.

The most characteristic art form in the Algarve and the rest of the country is ceramics. Most worthy of attention is not the pottery that clutters roadside *artisanato* shops, but the square, clay tiles known as *azulejos* which have been painted, glazed and assembled into decorative panels in Portugal since the

16th century. All types of buildings in the Algarve, old and new have some sort of *azulejo* ornamentation, none more so than the interior walls of churches where typically blue and white panels depict biblical scenes. In the days when it was a lot wealthier and more powerful in Portugal than it is today, the Roman Catholic Church also fostered the carving and gilding of wood on a grand scale. It commissioned stupendously ornate baroque altars and chapels which look incongruous now in churches with severely depleted coffers and congregations, or which have closed their doors to worship altogether.

Architecture

*T*he Roman Catholic Church has provided the Algarve with most of its most interesting buildings. All of the older ones have been damaged, repaired, pulled down, built up, altered, added to, renovated, restored, modernised or otherwise tampered with down the centuries. The same is true of castles and fortification walls. No really old structure has remained true to its original form. They have all undergone a process of evolution and taken on new

Portimão parish church.

Page opposite:
the church at Cacela Velha
was built in 1518 on the
ruins of a 13th-century
church, a small side doorway
of which still survives.

A roadside view of the outer
wall of the nymphaeum, or
water sanctuary, at the
Milreu Roman ruins, Estói.

A quiet corner of
13th-century Silves
Cathedral.

characteristics as events and needs dictated. The single most important event in the history of building in southern Portugal was the earthquake of 1755 which left no sizeable building unscathed. Fortunately the prime minister of the day, the Marquis of Pombal, was a man of formidable dynamism and resolve. He organised a massive reconstruction programme without which the Algarve today would have no interesting old buildings at all.

The first great builders in the Algarve were the Romans and there are several sites - near Estói, Vilamoura and elsewhere - where the remains of first and second century villas can be seen replete with baths and decorative mosaics . Nothing remains of the Visigoths and very little of the Moors. The oldest standing buildings built on Moorish foundations date from the Christian reconquest.

In the wake of the Arab retreat southward the Portuguese erected robust cathedrals as symbols of the Christian reconquest. The cathedrals of Coimbra and Lisbon, among the earliest in the country, are in the solid, fortress-like Romanesque style of the 12th century. The cathedral of Évora in the province of Alentejo came later. Built in the 12th and 13th centuries, Évora cathedral is an example of the transition from Romanesque to the more airy and majestic Gothic style. The Algarve's two cathedrals, at Faro and Silves, were originally Gothic and date from the mid-13th century. Both are small as cathedrals go, and are modest indeed when compared with the most imposing of Portuguese Gothic buildings, such as the abbey at Alcobaça near Leira in central Portugal. Characteristic Gothic features, pointed arches, buttresses and ribbed vaulting, can be seen in the parish churches of Santa Bárbara de Nexe and Loulé. Like Faro and Silves cathedrals, these two churches also have architectural influences from later periods. The parish church at Moncarapacho is basically Gothic but it has a renaissance doorway and a golden baroque shrine. The parish church on the high point of Portimão has been rebuilt twice, in 1755 and 1852, but the front portal remains pure Gothic. The twisted columns in local

*Manueline doorway
at Loulé hospital.*

*A detail of the Manueline
doorway of Alvor parish
church.*

marble separating the aisles of the parish church at São Bartolomeu de Messines are examples of the advent of *Manuelino.*

Manueline was a uniquely Portuguese style which followed the Gothic of the 13th, 14th and 15th centuries, but it remained in vogue for only a few decades before being taken over by the Renaissance. It was named after Manuel "the Fortunate" who came to the throne in 1495. Manuel was indeed fortunate, as were his subjects, for his reign coincided with Portugal's "Golden Age." Vasco da Gama discovered the sea route to India via the Cape of Good Hope in 1498. Pedro Alvares Cabral reached Brazil in 1500. Magellan set off to circumnavigate the globe in 1520. Meanwhile, Portugal's overseas possessions from Madeira to Malacca, from Ceuta to Ceylon, comprised a considerable chunk of the civilised world outside Europe. She wielded huge influence in international commerce, an influence out of all proportion to the Portuguese population of less than a million and a quarter. Lisbon was the focal point of world trade. Spices flooded in from the East Indies, sugar from the Atlantic islands, carpets from Persia, horses from Arabia, silk from China, silver from Japan, gold from India. With her empire safeguarded by supremacy at sea, Portugal's power and wealth soared. The glory and the prosperity which went hand in hand with discovery and trade was reflected in Portuguese art and literature. And there was money, plenty of it, to be spent on new buildings.

The excitement, exuberance and expansiveness of the period were given architectural expression most notably by four masters: Jean Boytac, Mateus Fernandes and the Arrudas brothers, Diogo and Francisco. They broke away from the formality and stiffness of the Gothic style by introducing flamboyant flourishes mainly on nautical or naturalistic themes. Stone columns fashioned like twisted ropes and sculpted motifs representing knots, anchors, chains, fishes, birds or plants are typical features of the Manueline period.

Surviving Manueline craftsmanship in the Algarve is

much less grand than that in places like Lisbon, Batalha, Setúbal, Évora and Coimbra, but there are some fascinating examples nevertheless. The main doorway of the parish church in Estómbar is one of them. The church's smaller side doors are similarly festooned with Manueline flora. More ornate still, are the Manueline doorways of the parish church in the village of Alvor, west of Portimão. Other fine examples of Manueline workmanship on doorways and windows can be seen at the parish churches of Monchique, Alcantarilha, Santa Bárbara de Nexe and the Misericórdia churches in Loulé and opposite the cathedral in Silves.

Above: Alte church detail.
Left: Main doorway of the church at Odeáxere.

45

The Manueline style, which was essentially florid surface decoration on late Gothic structures, gave way to the Renaissance revival of traditional, classical lines with emphasis on symmetry. The transition took place in the mid-16th century when Portugal went into decline as a commercial power. Costly over indulgence became inappropriate. But like the Manueline period, the Renaissance in Portugal was short-lived. The interior of Faro cathedral with its three naves separated by arches resting on Doric columns is an example of the renaissance style. The cloister of the Convent behind the cathedral was built by the renaissance master Afonso Pires. The portal of the São Pedro church with its fluted pillars is another example in Faro of 16th-century renaissance. Renaissance portals can be seen at the parish church of Alcoutim and the Misericórdia and São Paulo churches in Tavira. The church as Luz de Tavira is renaissance with Manueline pillars flanking the renaissance doorway.

The Reformation and Counter-reformation ushered in the period of baroque splendour. While the Protestants of north-western Europe disapproved of

The curious little chapel of Nossa Senhora da Rocha sits precariously on the clifftop site of a 17th-century fortress west of Armação de Pera.

46

all forms of ostentation, the Roman Catholic Church encouraged a bold, vigorous and exuberant style in architecture, decoration and art in the belief that it advertised the spiritual message and attracted followers. The baroque influence began in the Algarve in the mid-17th century. It was considerable, but confined mostly to interior decoration. At its most opulent it could be described as stunningly beautiful or outrageously garish depending on your taste in such matters. In Lagos the whole interior of the chapel of Santo António is an astonishing example of the baroque art of *talhas dourada* - intricately carved and gilded woodwork. The Carmo church in Tavira, plain on the outside, contains an almost mind-boggling display of baroque within. The São Francisco church in Faro is also plain on the outside, but inside it is a blaze of colour created by fine gilded woodwork, polychrome statues and pictorial *azulejos*. "Wild" is the adjective often used to describe the altar in Faro Cathedral.

One of the most imposing of all man-made structures in the Algarve is the mighty red sandstone castle at Silves. Like the smaller castles at Aljezur and

Bee-eaters over Silves Castle.

Paderne, Silves castle was established by the Moors who built on a site used by the Romans. The massive ramparts of Castro Marim castle envelope a 12th century castle ruin which was the first headquarters of the Order of Christ, the religious-military order which succeeded the famous Knights Templar.

Perhaps the most remarkable historic home in the province is the so-called *palácio* at Estói. It is not so much a palace as a once palatial country house built by the Viscount of Estói in the 18th century and grandly embellished in the 19th. With its terraces, gazebos, balustraded flights of steps, statues, grottoes and exotic gardens it has remained derelict and under lock and key for many years as a sadly neglected curiosity. Ordinary town and country houses built in the 19th and early 20th century are modest but distinctive in form. Local builders with a good sense of proportion, harmony and design constructed robust, rectangular houses one or two storeys high, rough plastered and whitewashed. Without the

Above and below:
front view of Estói palácio.

benefit of air-conditioning or heating, they remain cool in summer and warm in winter. The doors and windows are often highlighted with broad bands of colour, frequently blue. Lintel slabs of local rock are invariably used to create a similar effect on houses situated inland in the eastern half of the Algarve. Roofs are sometimes hidden behind horizontal screening walls which gives a squared off neatness to facades. In some houses the facades are completely tiled not only for decoration but with the advantage over whitewash that they are more resilient and thus not in need of regular attention.

Over the past 25 years or so, building has moved in three main directions: apartment blocks have been erected for local families, timeshare owners and tourists on package holidays; traditional townhouses and rural cottages falling into disrepair have been bought and renovated by foreign settlers; development companies have constructed large numbers of high quality "Mediterranean style" villas and apartments in

Some of the best modern houses retain traditional styles.

Above: An inverted triangle in a house window means there is a room to rent.

Below: Almond blossom.

complexes concerned with up-market tourism. Until 1991 there was a lamentable lack of proper land usage planning and building control with the result that infrastructures have been strained to the limit and the environment in places has been irreparably harmed. Eyesore high-rise apartment blocks in areas of natural beauty have given aesthetic offence while young Portuguese couples in particular feel the paradox of a shortage of affordable permanent housing and an overabundance of holiday flats standing empty for six or more months of the year. The authorities said they would not make the same mistakes as Spain and other Mediterranean countries, but they did. These mistakes now seem to have been recognised at local, regional and national levels. The need to protect the environment and the region's cultural heritage while at the same time fostering its social and economic well-being is the paramount task at hand.

Flora

The environment is made up of a wide range of habitats, including shifting dunes, sand flats, rocky shores, brackish wetlands, farmlands, dense woodlands, scrub covered hills and heathland. They support an intricate ecological web of vast variety which draws on Atlantic, Mediterranean and African influences. This combination produces a wonderful array of flora and fauna, including a few species unique to the region or rare elsewhere. Springtime is heralded in early January by pink and white almond blossom. In February the countryside is awash with it and joined by brilliant yellow mimosa (*acacia*), Bermuda buttercups and celandine. In February too, banks turn blue with *lithospermum* and periwinkles. Wild lavender and masses of rock roses add fragrance to hillside displays of grape hyacinths, scillas and aspodels in March. Bright blue borage is profuse in sandy soils alongside blue, pink and scarlet

pimpernels. Delicate irises share the roadsides with flamboyant burgloss and handsome crown daisies. In grassy and open stony places you find yellow bee, bumblebee, sawfly and mirror orchids. In April the lovely field gladiolus blooms rosy-crimson in orchards, yellow and red Australian tulips are plentiful on rocky hillsides and love-in-the-mists on sand dunes. The riot of botanical colour continues with jacaranda, Judas trees, broom, wild oleanders and a host of other blossoms and wildflowers throughout May and into June.

Swallowtail on gum cistus.

*M*ost spectacular of all is the avifauna. Almost 300 species of bird are resident, regular seasonal visitors or passage migrants. Little and cattle egrets, always conspicuous, are just two of the many species of special interest to visiting birdwatchers because they do not occur in northern Europe. White storks, which nest very publicly atop chimneys, and flamingos, several hundred of which spend much of the year in the Algarve when not nesting in the Cota Doñana National Reserve in Andalusia, prefer the eastern half of the province. Bonelli's eagles and ospreys nest on the cliffs of the west coast where short-toed and booted eagles, Black and red kites and occasional Egyptian vultures are most likely to be seen in passage. Red-legged partridge thrive on the *cistus*-covered hills. Purple gallinules, a rarity anywhere in Europe, may be glimpsed at the edge of protected reed beds near Faro. Black-winged stilts, raucous-voiced and unmistakable with their extra long legs, keep a high profile on salt pans especially in the breeding season. Alpine swifts, supreme masters of the air, nest all along the coast where there are cliffs and can be conveniently watched by basking sun-bathers. Bee-eaters, one of Europe's most dazzling birds, spend their time nesting in sand-banks and hawking for flying insects from March to September. Hoopoes, only a little less flamboyant, may be seen at anytime of the year, but are most common in summer. The dapper woodchat shrike perches like a sentinel on uppermost twigs and telephone wires while the outrageously vivid golden oriole prefers the privacy of plenty of foliage. Azure-winged magpies, unique in Europe to the south of the Iberian peninsula, feed in restless groups among stone pines. Commonest of all garden birds is the nervous and shy Sardinian warbler which is always on the move mouse-like amid bushes. Song birds such as robins, blackbirds and thrushes are extremely wary compared with their cockier cousins in the gardens of northern Europe. Perhaps this is because for centuries they have been persecuted with lime, spring traps and shotguns.

Birds

Hoopoes.

53

Animals

As with the flora, typically temperate zone mammals live side by side with semitropical species. Rabbits and foxes share common ground with genets and Egyptian mongooses. The genet is cat-like with a pointed face, short legs and a distinctive banded tail which is almost as long as its slender body and head together. By day it lies low in tree hollows and rock crevices. By night it hunts rodents and reptiles. The mongoose is often active around the clock in woodland, scrubland, rocky or even cultivated areas - the same sort of terrain genets inhabit. Unlike the genet which will climb trees, the ferret-like mongoose with its tapering tail is strictly a terrestrial creature. It is best known as an agile snake-killer, but it is also partial to all sorts of small animals and ground nesting birds.

Reptiles

One creature which has adapted extremely well to humans and the building boom of recent years is the Moorish gecko, a small lizard with adhesive pads along the whole length of its toes which allows it to

Ocellated lizard.
Photo: Margaret Daughtrey

scamper with ease on smooth vertical walls and across whitewashed ceilings. Virtually every house in the Algarve is home to a few geckoes. They come out at night in the summer to stalk insects by the light of electric bulbs. Don't let their appearance worry you. They are totally harmless to humans and exceedingly useful in that they can gobble up a great many unwanted mosquitoes in an evening. Geckoes are able to change their basic brown colour quite quickly, though they are restricted to turning lighter or darker as surrounding circumstances dictate. The real experts at this sort of thing, of course, are chameleons. The Mediterranean chameleon moves in characteristic slow-motion through bushes using its sticky, extensible tongue to snap up insect prey. There are quite plentiful in suitable localities, but it usually takes a lot of diligence and a sharp eye to spot one.

Encounters with any of the region's other lizards, salamanders, tree frogs, terrapins or snakes are best viewed with interest rather than horror. Nearly all are harmless and inoffensive. A few of the snakes are mildly venomous but will only bite if cornered and provoked, or in the unlikely event of being trodden on. Scorpions generally stay well out of harm's way in crevices and under stones. Stings are rare. In any case, far from being fatal, the sting of an Algarvean scorpion is about as potent as that of a wasp. The worst a visitor can normally expect from creepy-crawlies is an innocuous invasion by a line of ants making for scraps of food left lying around , or unwanted attention from mosquitoes which come out to bite at sunset. They can be a nuisance during the warmer months, but there are always simple deterrents available.

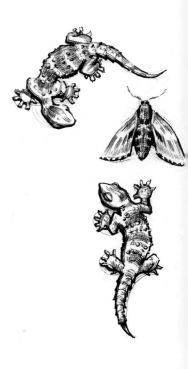

Egyptian geckoes size up their prey.

*A*n extensive breeding ground for mosquitoes was wiped out when the Algarve's first championship golf course was laid down near Alvor in the mid-Sixties. The 18-hole Penina course took the place of rice fields. It was designed by the late Sir Henry Cotton who ordered the planting of 350,000 trees to add character to the course and, even more importantly, to lower the water table. Sir Henry in later years was proud

Leisure

of the trees and liked to comment on the birds they attracted. He felt his course had been beneficial to the environment of the Algarve he loved so much. Whether golf courses help or harm the environment is debatable, but since the mid-Sixties a score more golf courses have been built or are presently in the process of being built. Instead of a problem of excess water, the concern now is to ensure sufficient supplies to keep greens, tees and fairways in tip-top condition.

Golf has contributed immeasuably to the expansion of investment, property development and tourism in the Algarve. All of the courses are associated with top hotels or villa holiday complexes. All are designed and maintained to a high standard and some are considered to be among the best courses in Europe. Taken together they offer a wide range of challenges in beautiful settings. To everyone's benefit, the main golfing season is during the otherwise relatively quiet tourist months of November to April.

Golf is the number one visitors' sport. There are good facilities for plenty of others: tennis, squash, horse-riding, athletics, lawn bowls, clay-pigeon shooting, archery, microlight flying and all the water sports including windsurfing, surfboarding, water-skiing, canoeing and sailing. Anglers have a choice of salt or freshwater fishing. Hours of leisure can be wiled away at waterslide parks where chutes with names like "the corkscrew" and "the kamikaze" guarantee unlimited squeals and splashes for the whole family, provided the faint-hearted members can be persuaded to come along too. For those with nothing more energetic in mind than falling into unruffled water in between applying layers of suntan lotion, there are countless swimming pools, public as well as private.

Finally, in the absence of anything better to do, you can always flop on a golden, sandy beach. There are more than 60 easily accessible beaches to choose from - and many others which may be all the more alluring because they are not quite so accessible. Sun worshippers, whether they enjoy solitude or the close company of hordes of other tanning torsos, will find in the Algarve the best beaches this side of - well - Paradise.

Page opposite: rainbow's end at the Quinta do Gramacho golf course clubhouse.

Central South Coast

From Faro to Albufeira

*F*aro, the Algarve's capital and largest town (population 22,000) is the point of arrival for visitors travelling by air. Planes approach over the Ria Formosa nature reserve, a large lagoon strewn with islets and sand-banks, to land at the Algarve's only International Airport. It is 4 km from Faro town. At the T-junction where the 3 km airport road meets the main east-west national road (N125), turn right for Faro and all places east. Turn left for all places west.

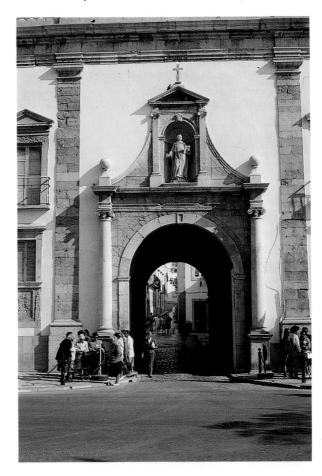

Arco da Vila, the main entrance to the oldest part of Faro, was designed in Italian style by a Genoese architect and dedicated to St. Thomas Aquinas.

The Roman town of Ossonoba was situated at or near Faro, but it was the Muslim Moors who gave it its present name and developed it between the 8th and 13th centuries. It was the last important town to hold out against the Christian reconquest, finally capitulating to the forces of King Afonso III in 1249. In 1596, during Portugal's 60-year subjugation by Spain, Faro was plundered and burnt by British troops commanded by the 2nd Earl of Essex, a favourite in the court of Elizabeth I. Essex made off with a magnificent collection of books which he donated to the Bodleian Library, Oxford - a decent gesture since he was educated at Trinity College, Cambridge. Faro was rebuilt only to be destroyed again by the great earthquake of 1755.

The Great Earthquake

*T*he morning of November 1, 1755 was bright and clear as autumn and winter mornings so often are in the Algarve. It was a Saturday but the churches were crowded: it was All Saints' Day, the Day of the Dead to the predominantly Roman Catholic population. The first and most severe of three massive shocks struck at 9.40 that morning. It lasted an incredible six to seven minutes and brought almost every church in southern Portugal crashing to the ground. In Lisbon it levelled 17,000 out of nearly 20,000 houses. The second shock hit at 10am, the third at noon. They caused landslides in the mountains. Huge sections of cliff fell into the sea. Fishing villages and town waterfronts were swept away by tidal waves. Some villages were submerged under 30 metres of water. Faro, along with towns like Lagos and Tavira, was devastated. The earthquake killed a total of up to 60,000 people. It was the worst earthquake ever recorded in Europe, reaching an estimated 9.2 on the Richter scale. Its effects were felt all over Europe and North Africa. Damage was reported as far away as Algiers nearly 1,000 km east of Faro. The German naturalist and explorer Alexander von Humbolt estimated that the total area shaken was four times that of Europe. The largest of the tidal waves reached England that afternoon and the Caribbean on other side of the Atlantic in the evening. Meanwhile in

The 1755 earthquake heralded the rise of the Marquis of Pombal as a national reformer. He went on to become a ruthless dictator whose tyranny ended with his own downfall two decades after the earthquake.

Arco do Repouso, the site of one of the entrances to Faro in Moorish times. Afonso III is said to have prayed nearby before his troops attacked the city in 1249.

Faro, Lisbon and elsewhere in southern Portugal, fires ignited by the earthquake continued to burn for six days. Many townspeople, fearful of more tremors, had fled to the open countryside. Those who remained behind searched for survivors and extricated the dead amid the threat of famine and pestilence. A special dispensation facilitated the prompt burial of bodies without religious ceremony. Other emergency measures were hastily introduced to provide food and shelter and to dissuade criminals from taking advantage of the situation.

It escaped no one's notice, of course, that Portugal's worst natural calamity had occurred on an especially holy day while thousands were attending Mass. This gave rise to a bitterly argued controversy : had it indeed been a natural phenomenon or was the earthquake an expression of divine wrath ? A side issue to the main debate was the uncomfortable fact that most of those killed had been devout Catholics at prayer, while the survivors included convicted sinners set free by collapsed prison walls. Fortunately, Portugal at the time had a strong and pragmatic leader in the Marquis of Pombal, formerly ambassador in London. Shortly after the earthquake he became chief minister to the ineffectual King José I. Pombal was less interested in what part, if any, God had played in the national disaster than in getting on with rebuilding shattered communities.

Old city centre

Little remains of pre-earthquake Faro, but the best way to get some insight into the town's past as well as its present is to take a stroll starting from Praça de Dom Francisco Gomes. This busy square is near the railway and bus stations and can be reached by car from the outskirts by following the *centro* signposts. With its obelisk and palm-shaded Manuel Bivar gardens standing next to a small boat basin, the square is named after the Bishop of Faro (1739 - 1816) who, in the same spirit as the Marquis of Pombal, did so much to restore the town after the earthquake. He commissioned the building of the Arco de Vila, a fine, Italian renaissance archway dedicated to St Thomas Aquinas, to replace a medieval doorway at the southern end of the gardens.

Page opposite: Cathedral Square, where Romanesque-Gothic, renaissance and baroque styles blend easily with the jet age.

The Arco da Vila (there is a tourist information office beside it) leads through the old, originally Roman city walls to Rua do Aljube which in turn leads to the cobbled Largo da Sé, Cathedral Square.

Faro's Romanesque-Gothic cathedral was built in 1251, probably on the site of a mosque and a Roman temple before that. It was extended and modified in ensuing centuries. Although some of it it survived the earthquake, it was badly damaged. The top portion of the tower collapsed which may explain its present stunted appearance. Inside, the cathedral is a mixture of Gothic, Renaissance and baroque styles. Many of the *azulejos* and much of the carved and gilded woodwork are 17th century. The red Chinoiserie organ just inside the front doors was made in Germany in the 17th and 18th centuries and was completely renovated a few years ago.

Cathedral Square with its 18th-century episcopal palace (opposite the cathedral) and town hall (by Rua do Aljube) is lined with orange trees. The statue in the south-west corner is that of Bishop Francisco Gomes. An even more imposing statue, that of Dom Afonso III who completed the reconquest of Portugal by finally liberating the Algarve, dominates the small, peaceful square immediately behind the cathedral. The king, sculpted in bronze, stands before the Convent of Nossa Senhora da Assunção which is more impressive inside than out. The convent was built in the 16th century and occupied by nuns for three hundred years. After the

Above: The old city's smallest gateway , Arco da Porta Nova, built in the mid-15th century to give direct access to the sea.

Right: a place to sit and sip next to the Manuel Bivar Gardens in Praça D. Francisco Gomes.

nuns moved out, the building was turned into a cork processing factory. In 1950 it became the home of the municipal museum. The cloisters, which survived the earthquake more or less intact and are worth seeing in themselves, are flanked by rooms exhibiting items of archaeological and artistic value. They include a 10 by 4 metre panel of 3rd-century Roman mosaics unearthed in 1968 during the laying of foundations for a new building in Faro's Rua Infante D. Henrique.

Azulejos

*O*ne of the galleries in the upper floor is devoted to *azulejos,* Portugal's most distinctive form of building ornamentation. *Azulejos* were introduced to Portugal at the end of the 15th century when glazed earthenware tiles were imported from Seville. Portuguese craftsmen did not begin making them until the following century, but it is known that by 1554 there were 206 potters and 32 *azulejos* specialists working in Lisbon. The tiles were predominantly blue (*azul*) hence their name, but in the 17th century yellows, greens and purples were added. The demand for *azulejos* became enormous. Early tile panels usually featured geometric designs, sometimes resembling Persian carpet patterns. In the 18th century the demand was mainly for large blue and white murals depicting biblical, historical or contemporary scenes. They were used to decorate both the interior and exterior of palaces, cathedrals and churches. In the 19th century their use was greatly extended and they commonly adorned municipal buildings, public gardens, fountains and ordinary homes. Hand-painted *azulejos* are still made, but the market has been swamped by mass-produced reproductions. The museum contains examples from all periods, including the earliest. Other than *azulejos* , the largest of the museum's many small galleries is filled with an extraordinarily diverse private collection of objet d'art and curios donated by a local dignitary, Dr Ferreira de Almeida. The picture galleries contain both old and modern works.

Leaving the museum and turning right, Rua do Repouso leads to the Arco do Repouso, another gateway in the old walls. Immediately outside the

Arabesque azulejos .

gateway and to the left, along Rua José Maria Brandeiro, a modern panel of *azulejos* at the side of the road shows the storming of Faro by Christians in 1249. Continue on through the Praça Dom Marcelino Franco with its eccentric Tribunal do Trabalho building, past Rua Alexandre Herculano, named after the most celebrated of Portuguese historians (1810 - 1877), and into Rua Manuel Belmarco where the old and new merge. One of the shops in Rua Manuel Belmarco specialises in Arraiolos carpets. Hard-wearing, richly coloured and usually elaborately patterned, these carpets are made by hand in the small town of Arraiolos near Évora 200 km north of Faro. The town's womenfolk inherited the craft from the Moors and have been stitching carpets, rugs and wall tapestries of high quality since the 16th century. From Rua Manuel Belmarco continue along Rua 1º de Dezembro and Rua Tenente Valadim through a crisscross of modern shopping malls with pavement cafes to Praça de Ferreira de Almeida, notable for its many inexpensive, typically Algarvean restaurants. Turn left into Rua 1º de Maio and you are back at the obelisk in Praça de Francisco Gomes.

Street cafe in a Faro mall.

*T*here are a few other places of interest on the fringes of this short walk. The harbour master's office, on the far right-hand side of the boat basin along from the Hotel Eva, houses a small maritime museum. Exhibits consist mostly of scale models of vessels such as the *São Gabriel,* the chief galleon in Vasco de Gama's fleet which pioneered the sea route to India in 1479. There is also a model of one of the huge and elaborate traps formerly used off Faro to catch tunny. There is a similar model in Faro's third important museum, the Musée Ethnographique Regional. Located in Praça da Liberdade not far north of Praça de Dom Francisco Gomes, the ethnology museum focuses on 20th-century everyday life and culture in the Algarve. Its bright and well laid-out exhibits are a useful primer for anyone interested in the traditional lifestyles which have been largely supplanted by tourism along the south coast, but which are dying more slowly elsewhere in the region. One of the items on display

Museums and Churches

Page opposite:
the renaissance cloisters of the former convent which now houses Faro's archaeological museum. The building was commissioned in 1529 and completed in 1561.

is the Algarve's last horse-drawn water cart. It is a two-wheeler which held a dozen big, earthenware urns. Before fresh water came on tap, Sr Manuel Inácio Miguel used the cart on his daily delivery round in Olhão. He delivered water door-to-door like this for 60 years and died in 1974 at the age of 97.

The church of São Pedro, along Rua José Estevão from Praça de Ferreira de Almeida, was originally a fishermen's hermitage. Built in the 16th century, it is richly adorned inside with 18th-century *azulejos,* and polychromatic and gold-leaf woodwork. Even more richly adorned is the interior of the twin towered church of Nossa Senhora do Carmo nearby. The Carmo church was inaugurated in 1719 at a time when great wealth was flooding into Portugal from Brazil. Huge quantities of Brazilian gold were used by Portuguese craftsmen to gild the intricately carved woodwork in a great many churches of which the Carmo church is an outstanding example. It is one of the most spectacular "golden" churches in southern Portugal. It is also the most macabre. A bone chapel (*capela dos ossos*) was built on to the side of the church in the early years of the 19th century. Inlaid into the walls and ceiling in geometric patterns are the skeletal remains of 1,245 monks. As you walk into the chapel you will see an inscription above the doorway. Translated it reads : "Stop here and think of the fate that will befall you."

The square in front of the Carmo church was the venue in 1722 for a fair to raise funds for the building process started in 1719. They continued to hold fairs here for the next 250 years. Nowadays, however, Faro's main fairground is the Largo de São Francisco, a huge dusty square outside the Arco do Repouso. Behind the plain facade of the church of São Francisco at the north end of the square is a dazzling display of baroque wood carvings, Italian-school paintings and *azulejos* showing scenes from the life of St Francis. The Franciscan monastery to the right of the church is now an army barracks.

The eastern side of São Francisco square overlooks the shallow Ria Formosa lagoon, a nature reserve of some 17,000 hectares. Enormous numbers of wading

Faro's Carmo Church, one of the most imposing baroque buildings in the Algarve. The first mass was in 1719 on July 15, a date still celebrated annually with a procession. The present building was completed in 1877.

birds stop here on passage between Europe and Africa during the spring and autumn migration periods. It is the winter haunt of big flocks of ducks. Resident and breeding species of particular interest to birdwatching visitors from the north include the flashy black-winged stilt, the Kentish plover which may be seen scuttling along almost anywhere there is mud, and the purple gallinule, a reed skulker.

Faro beach is on a long, narrow spit known as Ilha de Faro which shelters the western part of the Ria Formosa reserve from the open sea. The Faro camp site is here. To get to the beach and camp site (7 km from town) take the airport road, branch right as signposted just short of the airport terminal and cross the causeway at the end. Passenger boats ply between town and beach from June to September. By boat is the only way to reach the second beach in the area, Ilha da Barreta, a slender island which also forms part of the outer rim of the Ria Formosa reserve.

Ilha de Faro, a sand spit with a lagoon on one side, the open sea on the other, and a summer settlement in between. (Photo: Parque Natural da Ria Formosa)

São Lourenço

*L*eaving Faro, the N125 divides. A road branching left heads north towards the inland market town of Loulé (see chapter 6). Bear right if you want to continue along the 125 westwards. The first place of interest along the 125 is the church of São Lourenço de Matos standing on a rise to the right. It is one of the most remarkable of the Algarve's many remarkable churches. Its 18th-century *azulejos* cover virtually the whole of the interior walls and ceiling. The church is nearly always locked but as with most churches no longer in use, the custodian of the key lives nearby and will be happy to let you in if you find her and ask. A small donation towards the up-keep of the church is appropriate afterwards. Just down the road from the church is the Centro Cultural de São Lourenço, a German-owned commercial art gallery, one of the foremost in the region, which occasionally holds music recitals. Gunter Grass is among the regular exhibitors at the centre.

A covey of Algarve chimneys.

Church of São Lourenço.

Quinta do Lago and Vale do Lobo

Pinheiros Altos.

São Lourenço is on the outskirts of Almancil, a village once renowned for the diversity of its chimney pots, later a main road sprawl of restaurants and real estate offices, and now a busy little backwater by-passed by the 125. It owed its growth in the Eighties to its proximity to two of the region's oldest and finest privately developed resorts: Quinta do Lago and Vale do Lobo.

Set in 1,600 acres of pineland and lakes at the western end of the Ria Formosa reserve, the exclusive Quinta do Lago estate boasts one of the lowest building densities of any development in the Algarve. A new master plan made public in 1992, the development's 20th anniversary year, limits the potential population to just under 13,500 or less than 21 persons per hectare. Construction has taken the form of a number of small, high quality urbanisation built around central facilities,

most notably five golf courses. The urbanisations, with a mix of detached villas, townhouses and apartments, have been created and continue to be operated by some of the most respected names in international construction, including Bovis, McInerney and Trafalgar House . The five-star Quinta do Lago Hotel is managed by the Orient Express Group. Pinheiros Altos, the newest urbanisation within estate, in 1992 added yet another golf course bringing the total number of holes to 72. This has consolidated Quinta do Lago's reputation as one of the finest golf complexes in the Europe. The Portuguese Open has been played here several times and it is regularly the venue for celebrity tournaments. The superlative 18-hole São Lourenço course is kept by Forte Hotels for the exclusive use of guests staying at the group's Dona Filipa and Penina hotels.

The legendary Henry Cotton designed the course on the 1,000-acre Vale do Lobo resort which was founded in 1962 and continues to develop as an up-market villa and apartment complex. The golf course consists of three 9-hole circuits with narrow fairways rising from coastal cliffs through pine trees and orchards. The 7th hole on the yellow course is reputed to be the most photographed in Europe. It calls for a full-blooded, accurate shot across two spectacular ravines. Tennis *Vale do Lobo's famous 7th.*

enthusiasts are well catered for at the Roger Taylor Centre. Vale do Lobo is also the home of Barringtons, the Algarve's leading fitness and leisure club. It has a golf academy, squash and tennis courts and the Algarve's only cricket facilities.

Vilamoura

Vilamoura is the largest privately developed resort in Portugal and perhaps Europe. Its 4,000 partially wooded acres embrace three golf courses, a private airstrip, a marina visited by more than 30,000 boats a year and facilities for a wide range of other sports amid a plethora of holiday accommodation. The casino offers a glamorous night out, complete with an after dinner floor-show, for those who like to try their luck on slot machines or their skills at blackjack and roulette. Vilamoura's number one or "old" golf course is a British-style championship circuit of 18 holes with narrow fairways undulating through pine trees and giving fine views of the sea from elevated ground. It calls for extreme accuracy and is no place for beginners. Vilamoura II, formerly the Dom Pedro course, is an easier alternative. It is a flat 18-hole circuit in two contrasting halves: the front nine holes are open and within sight of the sea. The back nine are through avenues of pines. Vilamoura III has water hazards on eight of its 18 holes. It is a low-lying, sparsely wooded course which can be viewed in panorama from its impressive clubhouse.

The name Vilamoura means "Moorish village" but the area was inhabited long before the Moors arrived. In 1963 a local archaeologist saw fragments of Roman mosaics being churned up by a tractor ploughing on the north side of what is now the marina. Further destruction of the mosaics was halted and subsequent archaeological excavations have revealed the ruins of a Roman nobleman's house, extensive Roman baths, a factory or agricultural building, and a mausoleum or burial tower. The ruins have been fenced off but are open daily to the public. Roman, Visigothic and Moorish artefacts are displayed in a small, informal museum on site.

Vilamoura old and new... rare Roman oil lamp (top) and beer galore (below).

72

Quarteira

*Q*uarteira, fronting on the sea between Vale do Lobo and Vilamoura, is described in books of the Nineteen-sixties as "a pretty, little fishing village." All that has changed. The fishing village has been totally eclipsed by hotels and apartment blocks. Quarteira has spread both upward and outward and is now a high-density destination with the longest beachfront esplanade in the province. The beach itself, although narrow and punctuated by breakwaters immediately in front of the town, widens to the east and runs for some 20 km all the way back to Faro.

Quarteira and Vilamoura on the one hand and Albufeira with its satellites of Montechoro and Praia da Oura on the other, are the two most tourist-intensive hubs in the whole Algarve. Between them lie a couple of the Algarve's loveliest beaches, Falésia and Balaia, which are backed by a relatively sedate holiday hinterland with plenty of good accommodation. The famous south coast cliffs start at Praia da Falésia which stretches from the western side of Vilamoura, past the Hotel Alfa Mar and Aldeia das Açoteias complexes and the Pine Cliffs Golf and Country Club, almost to the fishing / holiday village of Olhos de Água. The Hotel Balaia complex presides over the wide beach of the same name. Between them, Vilamoura and the Falésia / Balaia area offer the region's best facilities for all sorts of land and water sports. Apart from familiar and

Quarteira's beachfront.

Vilamoura marina.

73

popular international sports, one of more restricted appeal is also prominently featured near here. As far as visitors are concerned though, it is a controversial and strictly non-participation sport.

Bullfighting

This is how it all ends....

Like it or not, the ancient and "noble" sport of bullfighting pits human skill, courage and style against the bull's speed, strength and aggression. As with any other sport it has well defined rules and procedures. Without a basic knowledge of these, it may appear to be a violent, incomprehensible shambles. Mind you, the same could be said of rugby or American football. Historically, bullfighting was run on similar lines all over the Iberian peninsula from at least the early Middle Ages until the beginning of the 18th century. The bulls were fought by knights and noblemen on horseback. It was the Bourbons in Spain who discouraged the aristocracy from risking their lives against the bulls. Tauromachy there became the sport of commoners fighting on foot. In Portugal fighting on horseback continued, but the horns of the bulls had to be sheathed in leather or tipped with metal balls. In Spain, the climax of a bullfight was the actual killing of the animal in the ring. This was forbidden in Portugal from the middle of the 18th century and was replaced by a purely symbolic kill. So it remains today. In the Portuguese version there is much less bloodletting and brutality, more variation in fighting technique with the main emphasis on horsemanship.

Bullfights are held near Albufeira from March through October - from Easter to All Saints' Day according to tradition. Tickets may be bought from agents in advance or from outside the bullring (*praça de touros*) on the afternoon of the *tourada.* The least expensive tickets are for seats exposed to the sun (*sol*) for the whole duration of the *tourada.* The medium-priced *sol e sombra* seats become shaded as the afternoon sun moves around. In summer, the always shaded *sombra* seats are best and the front row of the this section is best of all. None of the seats are cheap because the overheads in staging a bullfight are high.

For starters, there are at least two dozen principal human participants to be paid. Fighting bulls don't come cheaply either.

The bulls, one for each of the four contests which normally make up a *tourada* in the Algarve, are bred from pure Iberian fighting stock. They are carefully raised and selected especially for the ring, but the full extent of their fighting abilities will not be known until the day they are unleashed there. The quality of the whole bullfight depends on the quality of the bulls. A cowardly or docile bull will not strenuously test the skill and bravery of the bullfighters and will therefore produce a dull contest. No amount of waving red rags will stimulate a lethargic bull. Bulls are colour blind.

There are four types of bullfighter. Dashingly dressed in the style of 18th-century noblemen and mounted on superb, highly trained horses are the *cavaleiros*. There are two of them. They each fight

A novice cavaleiro about to place another bandarilha. Only bullfighters who have reached a certain standard are entitled to wear formal bullfighting attire.

Peões caping the bull.

one bull individually and usually they both fight the final bull of the afternoon together. The third bull is usually fought on foot by a matador or *toureiro* dressed in the customary "suit of lights." The other foot fighters in suits of light are *peões*, helpers whose main role is to distract or entice the bulls to take up certain positions within the arena. Finally, the least glamorously kitted out, are the *forcados*, a team of lads whose role it is to tackle and subdue the bulls with their bare hands after the *cavaleiros* have done their thing.

An afternoon at an Albufeira bullfight proceeds more or less as follows. At 4.30pm (later in midsummer) the men who will fight the bulls parade into the arena. They pay their respects to the public and to the president of the *tourada*, usually a local dignitary or official, who acts as a sort of grandstand referee. After this, the ring is vacated by all but the senior *cavaleiro* who limbers up his mount before taking up position opposite the gate from which the first bull will enter. His helpers stand at the ready with capes at various points around the ring just outside the inner barrier. The real action starts when the gate of the bullpen swings open and the first animal rushes out. During the bull's first charges, the *cavaleiro* is content to manoeuvre out of harm's way while assessing the virtues and vices of his adversary. Having taken stock of the bull, the *cavaleiro* then begins his *faena*. He asserts his command of the horse and mastery of the bull by planting a succession of short, barbed spears or *bandarilhas* in the bull's massive neck muscles. To do this he must repeatedly induce the bull to charge, and with split-second timing pass the horse within inches of the onrushing horns. It is usual for the *cavaleiro* to change horses midway through a *faena*, but it is unusual for either of the horses to be injured in any way.

A trumpet call signals the end of the *faena* phase of the contest and heralds the start of the *pega* featuring a team of *forcados*. While *peões* distract the bull with their capes, the *forcados* line up in single file across the ring behind it. When everyone is in position, the leading *forcado* shouts tauntingly at the bull which turns and charges. The first *forcado* takes the brunt of the attack. He gets hoisted off his feet and must then try to hang on to the horns while the rest of the *forcados* pile on top and try to bring the stampeding animal to a standstill. Not infrequently, bodies fly in all directions and the bull runs free. If so, the *forcados* must try again and, if necessary, keep trying until the bull is finally immobilized.

Once the contest is over, steers are brought into the ring to help herd the bull out and back to its pen. The bull will never fight in a ring again. Because of their remarkable memory, it would be both impractical and unacceptably dangerous to allow bulls to fight twice. Meanwhile, the *cavaleiro* and the leading *forcado* re-enter the ring to take their bows before the start of the next contest.

The second contest of the afternoon is similar in form to the first. In the third, the bull is fought Spanish-style. Its horns are unsheathed. During the initial charges the bull is caped by *peões* while the *toureiro* gauges its characteristics. The *toureiro* then takes over the cape work on his own. This is phase one and if the contest was being fought in Spain it would be followed by the lancing of the bull by a *picador* on a heavily padded horse. *Picadores* play no part in bullfighting in Portugal and so the bulls reach the *bandarilha* phase unhurt and unweakened. Three

Bullfights are well advertised.

pairs of *bandarilhas,* one pair at a time, are plunged into the bull's withers by an experienced helper or by the *toureiro* himself. To successfully implant the *bandarilhas* the bullfighter must run to meet the charging bull almost head-on, side-step at the last moment and reach over the horns. In the third phase, the *toureiro* establishes his dominance by performing a lengthy series of often graceful passes with a small cape called a *muleta.* Finally, with the bull standing still, head lowered in front of him, the *toureiro* simulates "the moment of truth," not with a sword as in Spain, but with a relatively harmless *bandarilha* or simply the outstretched fingers of his right hand.

The fourth contest is often the most spectacular. Both *cavaleiros* perform in the tight confines of the ring together, dexterously combining in battle and taking it in turns to place the *bandarilhas.* At the end, spectator reaction to this as with earlier contests depends on how good or bad the performances have been. Courageous bulls are warmly applauded. Inept or cowardly bullfighters are jeered. Bullfighters who have done particularly well walk proudly around the ring acknowledging ovations and picking up flowers and other objects thrown in by admirers. You can catch the action at bullrings in Vila Real de Santo António, Quarteira, Portimão and Lagos, but the busiest of all is at Areias de São João, Albufeira.

Albufeira before tourism.

A glance at the map of the Algarve shows that Albufeira is a medium-sized resort midway along the south coast. Albufeira is where you go if you like the close proximity of lots of other tanning torsos on the beach by day, and plenty of razzmatazz in the restaurants, bars and discos by night. The eastern or "new" part of Albufeira, is a stretch of undiluted tourist territory between the Montechoro complex and the beach at Praia da Oura. Beneath acres of holiday flats there are scores of watering-holes, shopping precincts and agencies renting or selling holiday flats. There are even holiday flats built into the bullring. This is a neighbourhood where you can buy British beer and cider on tap and where the karaoke carries on well into the night. Hangovers can be nursed with inexpensive full English breakfasts over which there is usually an on-going price war. Yes, take-away fish 'n chips wrapped in paper are available too. Hardly what you would describe as typically Portuguese in character, this new side of Albufeira sprang up from wheat fields and virgin land after the tourist boom got underway and the original part of Albufeira began to split at the seams.

Albufeira

Fishermen's beach.

"Old" Albufeira, a short drive or bus ride west of Areias de São João and Praia da Oura, is old indeed and over the past two millennia it has undergone several sudden and dramatic changes. Its origins are unknown but it seems to have been a fairly important place in Roman times. For the first few centuries AD it was known as Baltum and dominated by a Roman castle. In the 8th century, long after the Romans had departed, the Moors renamed it Al-Buhera, which roughly means Castle-on-Sea. They renovated the fortifications and during five centuries of security under Arab rule the town prospered because of its direct trade links with North Africa. When Christian forces attacked in 1189, they stormed both a thriving commercial port and a formidable citadel. The Christians occupied the town for just two years, only to lose it again to the Moors. It was not until 1250 that Al-Buhera finally capitulated to Afonso III's forces, most notably the Knights of Santiago . It was one of the very last Arab strongholds in Portugal.

The end of foreign rule also meant the end of foreign trade for Albufeira. With the severing of its

lucrative trade links, the town was plunged into poverty. It survived on income from fishing and hand-outs from the leading municipalities of the day: Faro, Tavira, Lagos and Silves. But it retained its castle which when visited by King Sebastião in 1573, five years before his Moroccan debacle, was well equipped with artillery to fend off attacks by Arab, French and English corsairs operating along the Barbary and Algarve coasts.

Albufeira was badly hit by earthquakes in 1719 and 1722, but worst of all by the one in 1755 which destroyed much of the castle and most of the other buildings in the town. The parish church collapsed killing 227 worshippers. Many other people drowned in a 10m tidal wave. In the year 1833 there was another calamity: the whole town was besieged and then set ablaze. It was the work of supporters of the usurper Miguel during the civil war, the so-called War of the Two Brothers. The most recent upheaval in Albufeira's chequered history has taken place over the past 25 years or so. The town, which so stubbornly resisted ethnic change in the 13th century, was among

the first in the Algarve to welcome the new 20th-century occupiers: foreign tourists. Holidaymakers have been instrumental in bringing about far more economic, social and structural change to Albufeira in the past 25 years than the Moors did in 500. The once prosperous Arab port and garrison town, which later endured 700 lean years as a humble fishing village, is back in business again having stumbled upon new wealth as one of Portugal's most famous holiday towns.

Albufeira today is a curious blend of old and new where the simplicity of yesteryear rubs shoulders with modern sophistication, and where the picturesque still manages to outshine the unsightly vulgarity of heavy commercialisation. Steep, narrow streets run down past stacked terraces of whitewashed dwellings to the town centre adjacent to the beach. Bem Parece on a knoll on the town's eastern flank commands one of the best overall views. Another is from the aptly named Hotel Boa Vista on the opposite flank.

To get a closer look and a general feel for the town, take a walk of less than a kilometre starting from the statue at the corner of Rua Coronel Águas and Rua 1º de Dezembro on the town's west side. The statue is of Vicente de Santo António, Albufeira's most celebrated son. He studied medicine in Lisbon and at the age of 29 he went with a group of missionaries to work in South America. Later, he entered the Augustinian Order and worked clandestinely as a missionary in Japan during a period of Christian persecution in that country. He was eventually arrested, imprisoned, then burnt at the stake in Nagasaki in 1632. He was beatified in 1867.

Next to the statue is the Church of Santana, but of greater interest is the parish church (Igreja Matriz) on the left a little way down the hill. It was built at the end of the 18th century to replace the original parish church demolished by the earthquake. Bishop Francisco Gomes consecrated the new building on July 15, 1800, eighteen years after work on it had commenced. The 28m high tower added in 1869 contains a carillon of eight bells. A little farther down on the right is the Church of São Sebastião built in

Page opposite: the statue of Vicente de Santo António.

The parish church.

1741 on the site of a chapel dedicated to the same saint. He was the subject of special veneration in the 17th century after performing some kind of "miracle" for the people of Albufeira.

Carry straight on through Praça Miguel Bombarda up to Praça da República and the oldest part of town. This is where the castle was located, but only vestiges of it remain. The "new" wing of the hospital on the left of Praça da República used to have a different type of inmate. Until 1975 it was the local gaol. Past the hospital on the left of Rua Henrique Calado is Albufeira's oldest building of note: the Misericórdia Chapel. Originally built in the 16th century in Gothic style, it has undergone many renovations. The Manueline doorway remains intact. Loop clockwise into lilliputian, time-warped Rua da Igreja Velha and then into Travessa da Bateria along which ran the original castle's southern wall overlooking the beach and the bay. The building on the right as you re-enter Praça da República used to be the town hall and has been

earmarked as a local museum.

Retrace your steps as far as Albufeira's longest-running quality hotel, the Sol e Mar, opposite which flights of steps lead down to Avenida 5 de Outubro. This is a mall of shops and cafes linked to the beach by a tunnel. There is a tourist information office and a post office at the bottom of the steps close to the tunnel entrance. Moving away from the tunnel, the first turning on the right leads to a square, Largo Eng. Duarte Pacheco, surrounded by bars and restaurants. This is old Albufeira's main focal point. Bear right along Rua Candido dos Reis, and you end up at the eastern side of Fishermen's Beach.

There are about 150 small fishing boats based at old Albufeira. They are between five and eight metres long with a characteristic high prow, brightly painted and bearing whimsical names like *Vamos à Sorte* (Go with Luck) and *Sempre Amigos* (Always Friends). You may also find a boat here named after the patron saint of Albufeira fishermen, Nossa Senhora da Ourada (Our Lady of the Oracle). The little church of this name is a considerable distance from the beach and not even within sight of the sea, but the fishermen go there in procession to honour their patron saint every August 15.

At ease on land and sea.

Fishermen's beach, known in Portuguese as Praia dos Pescadores or Praia dos Barcos, is amicably shared in summer by men mending nets next to their boats and by basking sun-bathers. Sun-bathers have the next beach along pretty well to themselves. It is called Praia do Peneco and it is reached through the tunnel built in 1935. Both of these beaches get very crowded. In fact in summer both by day and by night, Albufeira, old and new, is probably the busiest place in the whole province. There is a seaside holiday excitement in the air which repels as many people as it attracts. It's that sort of town: a dream destination for some, a nightmare for others.

Those staying in Albufeira who prefer quieter beaches should try those a little to the west. Baleeira is a clear-water bay, good for snorkelling. The Xorino Grotto is an interesting rock formation which can be reached by foot or on a boat trip. A bit further west along the road between Albufeira and Pêra, there are successive turn-offs to the São Rafael, Coelha, Castelo and Galé beaches which form a 10 km strand that runs uninterrupted to Armação de Pera, the next big resort along the coast.

Prow and prowess.

Western South Coast

*T*his section of the coast embraces two of the province's chief towns, Portimão and Lagos, and a dozen or so smaller towns and villages of special interest to visitors. No two towns or villages in the Algarve are alike. Each is remarkable for its individuality, for the uniqueness of its character and ambience. Portimão and Lagos have little in common with each other and are quite different from Faro and Albufeira, their rough equivalents to the east, or Olhão and Tavira, farther east still. Armação de Pera, Carvoeiro, Alvor, Praia da Luz and all the other places along the western south coast have characters all of their own as well. It is curious in this age of rapid and easy travel just how insular nearby communities remain. A Portimão fisherman told me he was born and bred in Lagoa. When asked if he often went back to Lagoa, he replied: "I haven't been back in 45 years." Portimão and Lagoa are separated by all of 8 km of good national road!

While Albufeira has been growing and modernising at an astonishing rate, Guia, the next village along, has remained as soporific as ever. It is famous for just one thing: barbecued chicken. It is a rather run-down place of a few hundred souls, but it enjoys this widespread reputation as one of the two best places in the Algarve to savour chicken barbecued with or without hot, piri-piri sauce. (The other place is on the road up to Monchique). Chicken, *frango* in Portuguese, is inexpensive and it tastes delicious anywhere in the Algarve, but Guia's reputation is such that Portuguese families flock here from a wide radius around. A few less hectic restaurants in Guia don't feature *frango* on the menu at all, but those which specialise in it are usually packed. Never mind the aesthetics, the atmosphere here is certainly a change from Colonel Saunders' establishments. A plate of olives and some fresh bread followed by a sliced chicken, a big plate of chips, salad and a bottle of wine shared between two is both

From Guia to beyond Lagos

cheap and filling. Piri-piri sauce, for the uninitiated, is finely chopped chillies in olive oil. It is best added before or during the cooking process but can also be added to taste afterwards. Incidentally, the main thing to remember if you are barbecuing chicken yourself is to get the fire right. Don't scrimp on the charcoal. Get a really good, lasting fire going. When the flames have died down completely, cook your chicken pieces slowly over the white-hot embers.

Alcantarilha

*I*f it is surprising that a place like Guia has managed to make its mark on the tourist map of the Algarve, it is more surprising that a bigger and more attractive

Above: former mule-drawn supermarket.

Right: former parishioners.

place like Alcantarilha 5 km down the road has not. Alcantarilha is strategically placed alongside the N125 adjacent to the eastern turnoff to the large holiday town of Armação de Pera. Until recently, a septuagenarian third generation wheelwright was turning out brand new working mule carts here as if Henry Ford had never been born. On the other side of the village, down by a brook which irrigates orange groves, local womenfolk still do their laundry by hand in an outdoor communal wash-house. It is a precursor of the automated, city launderette. It was built for villagers with no running water in their homes. Some villagers still use it even though they are now connected to the mains. Any of the women here will tell you that washing clothes in the fresh air and in the company of friendly neighbours is much easier than alone at a sink in the gloomy indoors. In the heart of Alcantarilha, in the vicinity of the parish church, most of the finest buildings have been locked, shuttered and left to decay like the contents of the church's bone chapel. Apart from a simple crucifix, the inside of this tiny chapel consists entirely of the skeletal remains of about 1,500 former parishioners. The walls and ceiling are covered with tightly packed limb bones interspersed with tiers of neatly aligned skulls. This is their final resting place after being exhumed from the church's original cemetery which had to be moved. The chapel was the only part of the Alcantarilha parish church left standing after the 1755 earthquake, though the bones are a comparatively recent addition. The church has retained Manueline

Most of the Algarve's windmills have now ground to a halt.

91

flourishes and the view from the belfry, if you can manage to get up there, is a panoramic one from the Monchique mountains to the sea.

Armação de Pera

It is said that Armação de Pera is of ancient origin and that it started out as a place where the farmers of Pêra, a village a few kilometres inland, kept their boats to supplement their income by fishing. Armação is now by far the bigger of the two. Indeed in recent years it has taken on a mini-Manhattan skyline and spread at a rate and style a bit like Quarteira.

There have been two major surges in Armação de Pera's evolution. The first was in the 18th century when a fortress was built. With a new sense of security the village spread around the fortress which occupied a prominent position above the beach and commanded a 180 degree view of the sea. One of the main functions of this fortress was to ward off attacks by corsairs. The infamous Barbary corsairs were government-commissioned privateers as well as freelance pirates who ranged out of safe havens along the north-west

Armação de Pera beach.

coast of Africa for centuries. Tripoli and Algiers were among their most notorious headquarters. So too was Salé close to Rabat just over the way from the Algarve in Morocco. The Barbary corsairs began terrorising shipping and harbours along the southern Iberian coast in the 16th century and greatly stepped up their activities in the 17th. Piracy flourished throughout the 18th century and it was not until the 19th that it was brought under control thanks to the efforts of the French and British navies.

Aspects of Armação de Pera.

Pirates of any complexion were generally not so much romantic characters as ruthless ne'er-do-wells. Rather than hold down steady seafaring jobs for meagre wages, they were recruited or forced to live dangerously by plunder with the promise of high spoils. The Barbary corsairs plundered not only material goods, but people. Abducted Christians were sold into slavery in Muslim countries. The Algarve's indented coastline with its concealing headlands and secluded coves would have been a happy hunting ground for lurking pirates had it not been for fortresses like the one at Armação de Pera. Sadly, this and similar fortresses along the coast have now all but disappeared through neglect. The Armação site, by the seafront road on the east side of the village, is marked by a modest fortress doorway with a coat of arms,

Successfully warding off pirates was one thing, but with the advent of mass tourism there was never any chance that hordes of holidaymakers would be kept at bay. Armação's fine location overlooking one of Portugal's longest stretches of drifted sand assured its popularity and its second major surge in growth. The growth in modern times has been westward. The livelier old section of the village, the east side, is where most of the cafes and bars are concentrated. Most of the big holiday apartment blocks are on the west side with a commercial area in between. On the western outskirts, two holiday developments, Vila Lara and Vila Vita Parc, enjoy a reputation for excellence. They overlook Praia Tramossos and a succession of coves along a craggy and particularly picturesque portion of

Singsong sailing.

The best ceramic plates, pots and panels are painted by hand and fired locally.

coastline. On a boat trip you will find some of the region's most spectacular sea caverns and grottoes. A tunnel links the twin coves of Praia Senhora da Rocha otherwise separated by a precipitous cliff on top of which, more than 30m up, sits a tiny chapel of unusual design. It is hexagonal-shaped with a pyramidal spire. This is the starkly simple fishermen's chapel of Nossa Senhora da Rocha (Our Lady of the Rocks) built in the 17th century when, no doubt, many a prayer for protection against pirates was said.

The western half of the road which loops through Armação de Pera has its junction with the N125 at the village of Porches. It is a tranquil old village best known for Porches Pottery, the Algarve's oldest working pottery, which sells hand-painted ceramics of good quality. There are a few other working kilns in the general area producing original ceramics - the Artlantico Studio near Lagoa for example - but nearly all of the household crockery, souvenirs and gift items on sale at scores of pottery shops all over the Algarve are mass produced further north in Portugal.

*E*ven though a great deal of the wine consumed locally is made further north too, the Algarve is an officially demarcated region producing six million litres of wine annually. Of the four official sub-regions (Lagoa, Portimão, Tavira and Lagos) Lagoa, 5 km west of Porches, is the most important. The vineyards which supply the Lagoa wineries are spread over an area stretching between Lagoa and Albufeira, Loulé and Silves.

During the winter months the wines, severely pruned back to gnarled stumps, lie dormant. In March they suddenly break into leaf and begin to grow rapidly. At this stage the plants are vulnerable to late frost which, though not common, occurs from time to time in localised pockets. Vines with enticing names like Negra-Mole, Periquita, Tricadeira and Crato-Branco thrive on the Algarve's stony soils and on the hot , dry, summer weather. Their roots go deep in search of moisture and nourishment. The last thing ripening grapes need is rain . Rain lowers the sugar content and may rot the fruit on the vine. So as the summer begins to wane, the growers keep an eye on the sky with some trepidation. The grapes are picked in September and early October and that is when you will see trucks, tractor-drawn trailers and mule carts piled high and heading for Lagoa's *adegas*. The largest of the *adegas* is the Lagoa Co-operative which is run on behalf of 350 member growers. The spacious parking lot around the building is empty most of the year, but during the second half of September and the first week in October there is usually a queue of vehicles waiting to have their loads weighed and fed into the presses at the start of the wine-making process. The Co-operative produces mostly red, but also white, rosé, fortified wines and a little aguardente. Visitors are welcome by appointment to look around the *adega*.

Lagoa has not much holiday accommodation but it is good for general shopping. Being a provincial town rather than a resort, it has a better range of shops and a less expensive morning market than Carvoeiro. Most of its restaurants too are less expensive than those closer to the coast. In May and early June, make your

Lagoa

A small winery at Carmujeira near Lagoa, and some of its produce.

way up to the parish church with colour film in your camera. The little square in front of the church will be ablaze with blue-purple flowering jacaranda trees. In August, visit *Fatacil* the Algarve's biggest open-air trade fair with its displays of arts and crafts, domestic and agricultural products, all amid a festive atmosphere.

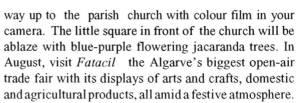

Top right: June jacarandas.
Above: sitting down job.
Top left: typical townhouse.
Right: pool with a view .

*T*he closest coastal village to Lagoa is Carvoeiro 5 km to the south. In a book published in 1965, South African-born poet David Wright said of it: "The mode of living remains essentially medieval, preserved by custom like a mammoth in ice." In those days there were few foreign faces in Carvoeiro. Then, suddenly, the local population with their medieval mode of living found themselves swamped by visitors from abroad. The tiny village, sitting compactly in a shallow ravine behind a cove flanked by low cliffs, spread fast and far as surrounding almond orchards gave way to modern, mostly foreign-owned villas. The villas are generally of a high standard and a great many of them have their own swimming pools. This is one of the Algarve's major self-catering holiday areas.

The Carvoeiro area abounds not only with private pools but with public beaches. Praia do Carvoeiro, on the village doorstep, is the most accessible, but not the most attractive for bathing. To the left and right of it, steep roads run up the sides of the flanking cliffs. Up the road on the right and around the corner, you will find a long flight of steps down to Paraíso beach. The

Carvoeiro

road on the left terminates at a small car park overlooking the sea-etched rock formation of Algar Seco. This is a good spot for snorkelling. The best places for bathing are farther east, at Centianes, Carvalho, Benagil, Marinha and Albandeira beaches.

Busy in summer, quiet in winter, Carvoeiro may find its tourist season extended somewhat with the opening of two new golf courses associated with the Clube and Monte Carvoeiro developments just west of the village. Some of the olive trees on the splendid double nine-hole Quinta do Gramacho and 18-hole Vale da Pinta courses were there in Henry the Navigator's time.

Portimão

To reach Ferragudo, the next village along the coast, you can take a slightly complicated back road route. Otherwise, from Carvoeiro return to the N125 at Lagoa and head for Portimão. Just outside of Lagoa you will pass a turn-off to Estómbar, a village which existed at least as far back as the Muslim occupation, but which is unremarkable except that the door of its church is a fine example of Manueline architecture.

Portimão is the Algarve's second commercial centre after Faro and its second fishing port after Olhão. It is not an immediately attractive town and although it is the sort of place which grows on you with time, few visitors are here long enough for that. Its main draw is its shops and markets.

Portimão appears on ancient maps as Portus Hannibalis. It is said it was thus named because Hannibal, the great Carthaginian general, led troops ashore here during one of his campaigns. Unfortunately, there doesn't seem to be a shred of evidence to support this even though it is likely that the Carthaginians had a settlement of sorts here. The Romans certainly did. So did the Moors. But in ancient and medieval times it was not nearly as important as the towns of Tavira to the east, Lagos to the west, or Silves about 13 km up-river. Situated on the west bank of the Arade river, Portimão's slow rise to regional prominence came with the progressive silting up of the Arade which in turn brought about the decline of Silves, formerly the Moorish capital of the Algarve.

Portimão tourist office.

Page opposite: pool privacy.

One of the biggest and best itinerant regional markets is held in the fairground next to the Portimão railway station on the first Monday of every month. It is a good place to buy inexpensive clothes, shoes and gift items. The marketplace is a short walk from the town's main shopping mall, Rua do Comércio, where consumer goods are generally dearer though of better quality.

One of Portimão's few buildings of note, the parish church, stands on the highest point of the town. Of the original 14th-century Gothic structure, only the portal survives. The church was totally destroyed by the 1755 earthquake, immediately rebuilt and then extensively renovated a century later. Its interior *azulejos* are from the 17th and 18th centuries. The oldest houses in central Portimão date from this period and are interesting for their tiles and elaborate wrought-iron balustrades.

The narrow streets leading from the Rua do Comércio and the area of the church down towards the river are good for shopping too. You will find high-quality crafted items in porcelain, pewter, crystal, embroidery and leather. Most of the best craftsmanship on sale here, as elsewhere in the Algarve, comes from central and northern Portugal. From near Aveiro, 500 km to the north, comes the famous Vista Alegre porcelain which

Fowl trade.

has been produced at a family-owned factory since 1824. They used to produce glassware also, but Portugal's finest glassware - full lead crystal - is made under the brand name of 'Atlantis' at Alcobaça, about halfway between Lisbon and Aveiro.

Largo 1° de Dezembro, a garden square in front of the court building which houses Portimão's tourist information office, has an interesting series of benches ornamented with 19th-century tile panels depicting 10 momentous events is Portugal's history from the founding of the nation on October 5, 1143 to the formation of the Republic on October 5, 1910. The Republic's first Ambassador to the Court of St James after the abolition of the monarchy in 1910 was Manuel Teixeira Gomes, distinguished patriot, writer and Portimão's most famous son. He held the post in London for 13 years before being elected President of the Republic, Portugal's highest office, in 1923. A plaque opposite the Banco Português do Atlantico on Rua Justice marks Teixeira Gomes' former home. There is a portrait of him chiselled in a block of marble at the centre of the fountain which dominates Portimão's most popular meeting place, Praça Teixeira Gomes, next to the river. His great-grandson, Dr José Manuel Teixeira Gomes Pearce de Azevedo, OBE, works nearby in the British Consulate. He has been the

Bridge business as usual.

Head porter.

Honorary British Consul in the Algarve since 1974 and was Vice Consul for more than eight years before that.

The Arade river is straddled by a railway bridge and two road bridges the newest of which was opened in 1991. Of the many reasonably priced restaurants in Portimão, among the most atmospheric in summer are those specialising in seafood on the quayside almost in the shadow of the old road bridge. This bridge, incidentally, was built in 1876 when most of the traffic around was hoofed, a fact best forgotten if you are stranded mid-river alongside heavy trucks and buses, feeling as if you are on a trampoline. The restaurants lost some of their atmosphere when the quayside activity of the local fishing fleet was moved several years ago to a custom-built wharf on the opposite side of the river. You used to be able to watch men working on the boats knee-deep in sardines, *carapau* or mackerel. They would scoop up baskets full of gleaming fish and toss them up to workmates on the quayside. It was a four-man, metronomic chain movement. The baskets would come up full and go down empty, their contents having been tipped into shallow, wooden trays and instantly smothered in crushed ice. The trays were then stacked into lorries and taken to markets and canneries. It was an age-old spectacle soon after the arrival of the fishing boats each morning and afternoon which always drew a crowd of onlookers. Then one grey day in February 1987 progress stepped in. All the fish arriving at Portimão are now landed, sorted, auctioned and dispatched from the restricted entry, computerised facility far from the public gaze on the other side of the river.

Fish bucket shop.

Ferragudo

Ferragudo, on the east side of the Arade estuary, has not yet lost its sleepy charm. Of its nearby beaches, Praia Grande inside the river-mouth breakwater is excellent for watersports. There is a camp site, a beautifully positioned hotel, some modest bars and restaurants scattered between the beaches and the village, and that's about it. It's quaintly rustic compared with Portimão's other beachside satellite.

Above: undercover operation on the quayside at Portimão.

Left: High and dry in a Portimão boatyard.

Below: Ferragudo.

Praia da Rocha

There are several little beaches tucked in between the cliffs and rocky outcrops between Praia da Rocha and Alvor....

This was the first resort along the Algarve coast to adapt to large-scale tourism from abroad and it has developed into a high-rise hive of summer activity with ample apartment accommodation and plenty of tourist-oriented activity by day and night. The beach, much of it reclaimed from the estuary bed by dredger, is vast. Unlike Ferragudo's Praia Grande, the beach at Praia da Rocha fronts on to the open sea. At its eastern end stands the clifftop Fortress of Santa Catarina. It was built between 1521 and 1557 by João III to protect the entrance to Portimão harbour. At its western end a tunnel called Buraco da Avô, dug single-handedly by a local man, connects the main beach with several smaller ones used by those who prefer greater seclusion while sunbathing.

Praia do Vau, the next main beach along the coast has the advantage of easy access, but finding a place to park your car may be difficult in summer. The cliffs peter out just before Praia do Vau but rise again immediately afterwards. Walking westward along the clifftop path, there are places where you can make your way down to isolated coves, or you may want to carry on to Três Irmãos and Alvor beaches which are better suited to children and the elderly.

Alvor

Alvor is one of those coastal villages in a state of rapid transition. Tourism has now taken over almost totally, but near the apartment and villa complexes there survives in the village proper a maze of narrow streets, lanes, blind alleys and one of the regions's most beautifully positioned churches. Alvor was founded long before the birth of Christ, maybe by the Carthaginians. There is speculation that Alvor, rather than Portimão, was the original Portus Hannibalis. The Moors called it Albur and several thousand Muslims were occupying it in July 1189 when it was plundered by Crusaders on their way to attack the Moorish capital of the Algarve at Silves. The attackers, under the command of Dom Sancho I, were less than thorough and the Muslims later re-took the castle. It was not until 1250 that the Christian conquest of Alvor became final.

On two widely separated occasions after that Alvor found itself at the centre of national and even international attention. King João II, the "Perfect Prince" who is generally regarded as the greatest of all Portuguese kings, died at Alvor Castle in October 1495 after a long illness and despite all efforts to cure him at the spa at Caldas de Monchique. He is remembered chiefly for his ruthless assertion of royal authority over the ambitious and at times treasonous aristocracy, and more particularly for his relentless championing of the quest for Prester John and a sea route to the East.

The earthquake of 1755 flattened Alvor. Although it was rebuilt, it was a shadow of its former self. And

Alvor is situated on the eastern side of a broad, sandy estuary and the coastline remains flat as it arcs around to Lagos. The Barlavento's characteristic cliffs rise again on the western side of Lagos bay.

Looking down the slipway and across the Alvor estuary to the Rocha headland , an ecologically important wetland area.

so it remained, a dozy village by the Alvor estuary. Patrick Swift in his 1965 book on the Algarve was able to sum it up in a single sentence: "Alvor, a flat open sandy stretch of beach, need not delay anyone, unless collecting shellfish has an interest for them." Ten years later, in January 1975, Alvor was chosen as the venue for negotiations which ended in agreement that the African territory of Angola should be granted independence on November 11 of that year, the fourth centenary of the founding by the Portuguese of the Angolan capital, Luanda.

Nowadays, Alvor "delays" a great many people in hotels and apartments overlooking the bay where village folk wade out to collect shellfish just as they have done since ancient times. While modern developments have eclipsed the post-earthquake village, the old cobblestone streets retain some of their quiet dignity and charm. The castle has gone, leaving the 16th century parish church as the village's most interesting building. It has a number of Manueline features, none more remarkable than the lavish main portal.

Many of the area's restaurants, places of entertainment and sports amenities are linked to hotels or apartment complexes, but there are quite a few modest eating and drinking places in the village itself and, during the warmer months, on the beach.

The wetlands associated with the estuaries of the Alvor and Odiáxere rivers, in the vicinity of the Quinta da Rocha peninsula adjacent to the village of Alvor are rich in bird life and have been at the centre of controversy for several years. Groups anxious to preserve the wetlands environment have been campaigning to keep developers at bay and to have the area proclaimed a permanent nature reserve. The area abounds with waders during spring and autumn migration, and studies have been carried out on its populations of breeding and wintering species. Black-winged stilts and little gulls breed regularly; there are many nesting pairs of fan-tailed warblers and Spanish-race yellow wagtails. Stone curlews breed here too but they are far more numerous in winter when you may be lucky enough also to see a Caspian tern or an osprey.

*A*t the western end of the bay which sweeps round from Cabo Carvoeiro to Ponta da Piedade lies the instantly likeable town of Lagos. It is especially popular among young backpackers and camper-van travellers. It's a lively but laid-back place. It is easy-going nowadays, but it has not always been so. Incredible as it may seem today , Lagos was once at the very fulcrum of earth shattering events.

Carthage had a far-flung outpost in Lagos well over 2,000 years ago. The Romans penetrated the Carthaginian walls and set up their own settlement, probably in the half century before Christ. Lacobriga as

Lagos

Lagos' Pau da Bandeira fort.

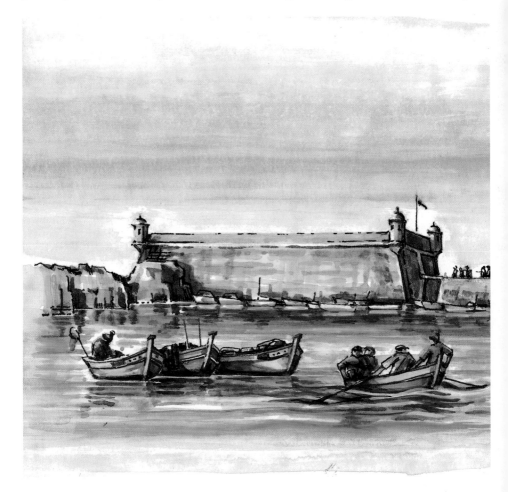

Lagos' Rua 25 de Abril.

Gil Eanes, Lagos' most famous son, broke a forbidding physical and psychological barrier by rounding Cape Bojador in West Africa in 1434.

it was then called was nurtured by the Moors as an important trading link between Portugal and North Africa. This ended with the reconquest in 1249. Long after they had expelled the last of the Moors from the Algarve, the Portuguese continued to attack the Muslims on their home territory. In 1415, a mighty fleet of Portuguese galleys assembled in Lagos Bay just before the invasion of Ceuta on the north coast of Morocco. This invasion, a manifestation of Portugal's Christian preoccupation with harrying the "infidels," turned out to be a prelude to Portugal's "Age of Discovery" which dramatically redefine Europe's perception of the world. One of the key figures in the Ceuta invasion and the prime mover behind the Discoveries was the Infante Dom Henrique, Prince Henry, better known as Henry the Navigator. Lagos was where he had his ships built, refitted and victualled for the great voyages which began tentatively down the coast of north-west Africa in 1419 and culminated with Vasco da Gama's epic voyage in 1499. There is a bronze statue of Henry in the Praça do Infante, shown on some tourist maps as Praça da República. It is a good starting point for a short walking tour of the town.

Henry the Navigator was half English. Born in Oporto in 1394, he was the third surviving son of King João I and Philippa of Lancaster, John of Gaunt's daughter. He was just 21 when he distinguished himself as a military commander in the 1415 conquest of Ceuta. Four years later, he was appointed governor of "the Kingdom of Algarve." This is where he stayed for the remaining 41 years of his life, probably dividing his time between overseeing operations in the then illustrious port of Lagos, and master-minding further overseas exploits at his so-called School of Navigation at Sagres. His bronze statue, mounted on a marble plinth, was erected here in 1960 on the 500th anniversary of his death. He is holding an astrolabe, an early navigational instrument. The square here is paved with dark and light coloured *calçadas* in a wave-like pattern.

Walk over to the left to the renovated town walls. In a corner, quite high up, you will see a small window fringed with elaborate, Manueline ornamentation. It is said that King Sebastião addressed his troops from this window just before setting out from Lagos in 1578 on the disastrous expedition to Alcacer-Quivir in Morocco. Follow the castellated walls away from the Praça do Infante until you reach another bronze statue. This is of Gil Eanes, one of Henry's most distinguished captains. He was born in Lagos and in 1435 made a momentous breakthrough as the first European to round the forbidding Cape Bojador on the west coast bulge of Africa. The statue was erected on the 550th anniversary of this feat.

Nearby, in the tunnel through the town walls, there is a small shrine unveiled in 1942 to commemorate the 500th anniversary of the death of the Algarve's only saint, São Gonçalo de Lagos, a fisherman's son born locally in 1360, who entered the Augustinian Order and became an outstanding preacher and religious writer credited with several miracles. At the end of the tunnel, turn sharp right into the Rua do Castelo dos

Pau da Bandeira fort, front and back

Lagos Museum is a short walk through the centre of town from the main avenue lined with palm trees next to the harbour front.

Governadores. On the right is the local hospital which stands on the site of the palace residence of a succession of governors who administered the Algarve for the 200 years Lagos was the provincial capital prior to 1756. At the far end of this street, also on the right, is the church of Santa Maria.

The Santa Maria Church and the tombstone fragments at its entrance date from the 16th century, although it was substantially rebuilt in 1848. Redecoration work carried out over the past decade has included the painting of a mural behind the altar by a English mystical artist, Ken Ward. On your left as you leave the church is a 17th- century regimental storehouse, now used for arts and crafts exhibitions and an annual racing pigeon show.

Take the street to the left of the storehouse, Rua Henrique Correira da Silva, which leads to the church of Santo António and the regional museum. Both are remarkable. Go round the corner and into the museum first. There is a small charge, but it is worth it. The museum is split into little galleries housing items of archaeological as well as regional and ethnographic interest. There are weapons, a numismatic section, freak biological specimens pickled in jars, and a gallery devoted to sacred art, including garments worn at the Mass just before the departure for Alcacer-Quivir.

From the museum you emerge into the extraordinarily ornate church of Santo António, a masterpiece of gilded carving. It was rebuilt in 1769. The blue and white *azulejos* panels depicting scenes form the life of St Antonio were made by a Loulé artist after the 1755 earthquake. Rather incongruously, a tombstone on the floor of the church is engraved with the name, Hugo Beatty. He was an Irishman, the commander of a local regiment, who died in 1789.

Sebastianism

Our walking tour now takes us along Rua 25 de Abril, probably Lagos' best street for restaurants, bars and cafes. It also has some interesting shops. It leads to Praça Gil Eanes which features a statue of Sebastião, the 16-century boy ruler who made such an extraordinary impact on his subjects. The statue is by the much acclaimed Lisbon artist, João Cutiliero. It was unveiled in 1973 and has been the subject of ridicule ever since. The wide eyed, pink faced youth in armour has been likened in guidebooks to "a mod motor-cycle rider" and "something from a science fiction movie." Another uncharitably says Sebastian looks like "a flower-pot man" and dismisses the statue as "fantastically dreadful."

Sebastião, the man and the myth, has always evoked strong emotions. He seems to have been an obstinate, self-opinionated and fanciful youth who became king in 1568 at the age of 14. He first came to the Algarve

Above: Ponta da Piedade.
Left: girl and the boy king.

in 1573. The proximity of the province to North Africa is said to have greatly excited his crusading desire to exterminate Muslims in their heartland. He raised an army of Portuguese, German, Dutch and Spanish troops and adventurers who set off from the Algarve in a fleet of 500 ships in June 1578. The expedition was hopelessly ill-conceived and doomed from the start. Once in Morocco, the foot soldiers and horsemen, accompanied by several thousand servants, priests and prostitutes, soon ran out of provisions and lost contact with the fleet which was their lifeline. At Alcacer-Quivir, suffering from hunger and heat exhaustion, they were surrounded by a vastly superior Muslim army. Eight thousand of Sebastião's followers were slaughtered, 15,000 were captured and only a few hundred escaped. Sebastião was among the dead, but at home many refused to believe it. Some thought he was on an extended pilgrimage; others accepted he had died, elevated him to Messiah status and awaited a second coming. They waited and waited blissfully unaware that all their hero had done was ensured the demise of the 200 year old House of Avis, an illustrious line of succession which had begun in 1383 with João I. Sebastião's only heir was his elderly and celibate great-uncle, a cardinal. The Portuguese crown was therefore soon up for grabs. The man who grabbed it was Philip II of Spain. Thus began Spain's 60-year annexation of Portugal.

Page opposite: Portugal's crusading ships carried the cross of the Order of Christ.

Lagos' coat of arms in front of the town walls near Sebastião's window.

Slavery

*H*aving approached Sebastião from the rear, so to speak, do what he should have done in Morocco and make a U-turn. You will find Rua da Barroca on your left. It is a narrow walkway flanked on one side by a melange of small houses and a few restaurants. It turns into Travessa and later Rua da Sra. da Graça which slopes down to the north-east corner of our starting point, Praça do Infante. Here, on the corner on the right-hand side, you will find a tiny art gallery with a railed forecourt. This was Europe's first slave market. Henry the Navigator found that trading in slaves was a convenient way to help finance his costly voyages of discovery. In the beginning, slaves were obtained from the coastal areas of Africa west of the

Ingrina.

Burgau.

Sahara by Portuguese seamen who raided villages and forcibly dragged off their human booty. Later, a peaceful and increasingly brisk and lucrative barter trade was established with the full co-operation of tribal chiefs and local headmen. Slaves, often captives from inter-tribal fighting, were gladly exchanged for cloth, corn or brassware. The estimated number of slaves brought back to Portugal in the second half of the 16th century was around 150,000. In the following two centuries the number increased dramatically. The Portuguese had competition from the Spanish, French, Dutch and - more than anyone - the British.

The Portuguese slave trade was facilitated by a string of forts along the African west coast and by ships specially fitted out for bulk human cargoes. Slaves were bought, herded, transported and sold like cattle. They were put to work extensively in southern Portugal and on Portugal's Atlantic island colonies. In the 16th century, the majority of West African slaves provided the labour force for the sugar and tobacco plantations in Portuguese Brazil. By the last quarter of the century Angola, rather than Guinea and other countries in north-west Africa, had become the main source of slave labour.

By the start of the 17th century, Sudanese slaves were in greatest demand because they were said to be more robust. They were considered ideally suited to working the Brazilian gold mines. Christian justification for all this was found in biblical texts. It was satisfying to know that while savage bodies were enslaved, their heathen souls could be saved. Few voices were raised in protest during the three centuries and more that the slave trade flourished in Portugal. Few people nowadays, least of all authorities promoting tourism, are keen to glorify those days. The slave market in Lagos is thus not much to look at.

There is a variety of excellent beaches in the Lagos area starting with Meia Praia, a long, sandy beach reached by a turnoff on the east side of the bridge which spans the Bensafrim river. More popular and more spectacular are the beaches on the other side of the town, starting from the 17th-century fortress at the mouth of the harbour. You can make your way on foot from Batata and Pinhão beaches round to Praia D'Ana and on to Ponta da Piedade passing an extraordinary profusion of coves, caves, tunnels, grottoes, stacks and beautifully coloured and weirdly weathered cliff-faces. About 400 pairs of cattle egrets and little egrets nest in mixed colonies on the stacks of Ponta da Piedade. From the lighthouse on the point, you have a panoramic view on a clear day from Cabo Carvoeiro on the left, all the way round to the headland at Sagres on the right. For some, the only drawback about this sensational stretch of coastline is that it naturally attracts a lot of people in summer.

For a quieter, more village-like atmosphere, travel on westwards from Lagos to Praia da Luz (6 km), Burgau (12 km) and Salema (19 km). Each is situated by a broad cove with a walk-on beach. All three have plenty of holiday apartments and there are camp sites at Praia da Luz and Salema. A bus service connects the villages with Lagos. Those with their own transport and a preference for more isolated beaches should motor on to the village of Raposeira where there is a signpost to Ingrina and Zavial. By then you are beginning to savour the special delights of the Algarve's west coast.

South-west beaches

Above: Zavial.
Below: end of the line.

Eastern South Coast

From Vila Real to Olhão

*V*ila Real de Santo António on the Guadiana river was long the gateway town for travellers between the Algarve and the Spanish province of Andalusia. With the opening in 1991 of a bridge across the river a short distance upstream, and the easing of immigration and customs formalities, Vila Real's importance has diminished, especially for passing vehicular traffic. However, ferry boats still regularly ply between Vila Real and its Spanish counterpart on the opposite side of the river, Ayamonte. It is an inexpensive, 15 minute trip. The ferries carry passengers and all types of vehicles. The frontier checks, bus terminus, railway station, tourist office and exchange bank are all conveniently close to the ferry quay. The town itself is unique in the Algarve in that its streets are all laid out in a grid pattern. It was planned and built, virtually from nothing in a matter of months midway through the second half of the 18th century, under the direction of the Marquis of Pombal. He wanted an efficient, economical fishing town modelled on the Baixa district of Lisbon. It has not changed much in appearance despite the large number of international visitors who pass through it each year. The main square, a spacious *praça* flanked by elegant 18th-century houses, still bears the Marquis' name. Incidentally, the abbreviated version of Vila Real de Santo António's name is often used in the Algarve, but it is not to be confused with the city of Vila Real in northern Portugal.

Frontier fortifications.

Castro Marim

*T*he nearby town to the north, Castro Marim, is smaller than Vila Real de Santo António, but it has a much more illustrious history. It came into considerable prominence in the early 14th century with the abolition, under pressure from Philippe le Bel of France, of the Knights Templar who had fought for the best part of 200 years against the Muslims in Europe. Portugal went along with the suppression of the international Templars because of their alleged heinous crimes, but it allowed

Page opposite: storks and swallows are common in the eastern Algarve and are not shy of carrying out their domestic duties in public. ·

117

it allowed them to re-emerge almost immediately in a slightly different form calling themselves the Order of Christ. This new religious military order was purely Portuguese. It was founded in 1318 by King Dinis in conjunction with Pope John XXII. The place chosen for its first headquarters was Castro Marim. The initial role of the new order was the defence of the Algarve over which there was a running territorial dispute between Portugal and neighbouring Castile. But the Moors also remained a threat in the 14th century for although they had long been defeated in the Algarve, the reconquest was not yet complete in Spain. So when the soldiers of the Order of Christ moved into Castro Marim it was already a place of great strategic importance. Like the Romans and the Moors before them, the medieval Portuguese maintained a mighty fortification here. It is not difficult to see why they chose this spot if you walk or drive up to the castle ruins which still loom over the little town today.

The Guadiana estuary beyond the ramparts of Castro Marim castle.

Castro Marim castle's hilltop position commands unobstructed views all around over a wide radius. In particular, it overlooks the estuary of the Guadiana with its broad alluvial valley and fenlands. Over the years, the river has meant different things to different peoples: a source of food and irrigation, a waterway to inland deposits of copper and tin, a sheltered anchorage. More than anything, though, it has been a natural frontier over which a careful watch was constantly kept for invaders. The castle from which the men of the Order of Christ kept vigil was square with a cylindrical tower at each of its corners. Today, it stands in a badly renovated state within a later and much larger castle which continued to be one of Portugal's most important military installations until the 17th century. Besides the "old" inner castle, the outer ramparts encompass the remnants of a variety of buildings ranging from an Iron Age mill to a mid-17th century gunpowder store.

São Sebastião Fort. was commissioned in 1641.

The castle is on the eastern or river side of the road through Castro Marim. Its decline as a military stronghold dates from the 17th century when a plush new citadel was constructed on a hilltop on the other side of the road. This is the Fort of São Sebastião built by King João IV who is best known for restoring Portugal's independence after six decades of Spanish annexation. The new fort was designed to help ensure continued independence from threats from the other side of the river.

So, above all, Castro Marim is a place of castles. It is also a place of churches. There are two within the compound of the larger fortress, although only one is in good enough state to be easily recognised as such. This is the Igreja de Santiago (St James'), a much restored 14th-century church where Henry the Navigator worshipped during visits to Castro Marim in his capacity as Grand Master of the Order of Christ. The most interesting features to have survived the restoration work are the portal and a couple of tombstones dated 1628 and 1634. From the castle battlements you can easily spot the domed 18th-century Igreja da Nossa Senhora dos Martires on the south or seaward side of the town. In the shadow of the castle on the west side stands the main parish church, also domed. A short

Castle within a castle.

The Castro Marim nature reserve is the best place to look for flamingos (below). Flocks of them can often be seen feeding in shallow waters in the company of other aquatic species such as avocets (above).

walk away, at number 53 Rua 25 de Abril, is the town's smallest place of worship, a mini chapel with a tiled facade. Notice the pyramid shaped roof, an architectural feature characteristic of the eastern Algarve.

Most of Castro Marim's population of 4,000 live in spick and span terrace cottages with ornamental flourishes to proclaim individuality. It is fashionable to outline windows and doorways with broad painted bands, not in drab or traditional colours but in paint-box delicate pastel hues or paint box shockers. This does not mean that historic Castro Marim is entering a swinging age. There is neither beach nor boutique. There is no hotel or camp site, no estate agencies or night-spots. Castro Marim leaves that sort of thing to nearby Monte Gordo. There is, however, a large nature reserve of special interest to botanists and birdwatchers. More than a hundred species of plant are found in the reserve which includes big areas of brackish fenland as well as commercial salt pans. Of the many species of

waterbirds, the most distinctive is the flamingo which visits in flocks from its nearest breeding grounds in Spain's Cota Donaña national park. Maps of the Castro Marim reserve and an outline of what species you can hope to see there may be obtained from the Castro Marim office of the national parks and reserves service. The office is just inside the gate of the main castle.

Monte Gordo is the first of the Algarve's beach resorts for those travelling from the east. One of its big attractions for Spanish visitors is its beachside casino, but its most remarkable feature is the beach itself. It is massive. In summer it is colourfully crowded mainly by folks from Spain and Lisbon. Backed by woods of stone pine, the beach stretches westward through the smaller and quieter resorts of Praia Verde, Alagoas and Manta Rota. It carries on as a sandbar past Cacela Velha as far as Cabanas making it an uninterrupted stretch of golden sand almost 20 kilometres long.

Cacela Velha

*T*he Algarve is so steeped in history that even a one donkey hamlet like Cacela Velha has had its moment of glory. With its small fort, church and a few cottages overlooking a wide sweep of lagoon within the Cacela - Cabanas sandbar, Cacela Velha is of great antiquity. But its niche in history was secured comparatively recently: in June 1833. The Peninsular War (1808-1814) with its devastating Napoleonic invasions of Portugal and the ensuing British occupation, together with the spread of democratic ideas as a consequence of the French Revolution, all created a climate of discontent and agitation in Portugal. The Portuguese Revolution, which began in Oporto in 1820 and quickly spread to Lisbon, signalled the start of a long period of political upheaval. To this was added economic strife following Brazil's declaration of independence in 1822. The country found itself divided. On the one side were the Liberals who supported a democratic constitution similar to that in Britain. On the other were the Conservatives or Absolutists who wanted to preserve the old ways and maintain strong royal authority. The Liberals rallied

The fort and the lagoon.

121

around Dom Pedro IV who, in order to retain the throne of Brazil, abdicated the Portuguese crown in favour of his seven-year-old daughter, Maria da Glória. The Absolutists supported Dom Pedro's younger brother, Miguel, Maria da Glória's regent, who seized power and was declared king in July 1828. The Liberals withdrew to the Azores, but within three years Pedro was ready to make a comeback. He abdicated the Brazilian throne and came to Europe to raise men and money to move against the Absolutists. In July 1832, a Liberal fleet sailed from the Azores and occupied Oporto, but the rest of the country remained Absolutist. The turning point came the following summer when the English admiral, Charles Napier, took command of the Liberal Navy. Although well out-gunned, Napier defeated the Miguelite navy off Cape St Vincent and sailed on to put 2,500 troops ashore at Cacela Velha. These troops, under António José de Sousa Manuel, Duke of Terceira, advanced by way of Tavira and Lagos on Lisbon. When they reached the capital they found it had been abandoned by the Miguelite forces. Within 10 months the Absolutists had capitulated throughout the country. The War of the Two Brothers ended with Miguel being forced into exile. Pedro died shortly afterwards. Maria da Glória became Queen Maria II at the age of 15. Napier, "Mad Charley" as he was known to his subordinates, was awarded a knighthood in England and created Conte Napier de São Vincente in the Portuguese peerage. Three years after the Cacela beachhead, he rejoined the British Navy where it was said of him: "He is not to be trusted except in the hour of danger, and then he performs prodigies far beyond all calculation." His hero's image was to take a severe tumble two decades late during the Crimean War. As commander of Britain's Baltic Fleet, he refused to attack the great Russian naval base of Kronshtadt, claiming that he did not have enough firepower. It was not something that had worried him off Cape St Vincent.

Pictured opposite: The church of Santa Maria do Castelo, the most distinctive and historically important of Tavira's main churches. Although the 13th-century original has been much renovated, some of its Gothic features have been preserved. An Arab-style window on the left of the clock tower recalls the church's earlier incarnation. Before the Christian reconquest it was a mosque.

Below: The much renovated 16th-century church at the busy eastern Algarve village of Moncarapacho has a fine renaissance portal.

Tavira

*T*avira, with its relaxed and well-worn ambience, is considered by many to be the most pleasant and picturesque town in the Algarve. It is also one of the oldest. At one stage, it was the largest. The Romans built a seven-arched bridge which links the two halves of the town by spanning the normally placid river Gilhão. The bridge was on the well used Roman road from Faro to Mertola. The Moors surrendered here in 1242 and the tomb of the commander of the conquering Portuguese forces is preserved in one of Tavira's 37 churches. A plaque on the bridge recalls that a Castillian invasion was halted at the river in the 14th century. By the 15th century, Tavira had become a commercial port of considerable size, wealth and

Praça da Republica.

Right: view from the castle.

importance. Up to 70 merchant ships lay in its harbour at any one time taking on salt, wine and dried fish for export to north-western Europe and Africa. It was the gradual silting up of the Gilhão that brought about Tavira's demise as a trading port. Much more recently, an unexplained change in the migration route of the tuna shoals brought about its downfall as a fishing port. Despite all this, there is still much of interest here.

The focal point of the town is the Praça da República. It is on the west side of the seven-arched bridge which was badly damaged by floodwaters in November and December 1989. One side of the square is taken up by a long, arcaded building. This is the town hall. It houses the local tourist information office. On the east corner of the building you will notice a mask carved into the wall. It is believed to represent Dom Paia Peres Correia who conquered Tavira and much else in the Algarve. Immediately across the road, through an archway and up a few steps is the Misericórdia Church, originally built in 1541, with its renaissance doorway surmounted by statues of St Peter, St Paul and Our Lady of Mercy.

A church tower almost nice enough to eat.

The word *misericórdia* crops up frequently in Portugal, often in connection with specific churches. The Santa Casa da Misericórdia, Holy House of Mercy, was founded under royal patronage in 1498 as a charitable lay brotherhood. Members, whether from the gentry or the working class, had to be "men of good conscience and repute, walking in fear of God, modest, charitable and humble." It was essential that they had "purity" of blood without any "taint" of Moorish or Jewish origin and that they were comfortably enough off so as not to be tempted to embezzle funds. The duties of the brotherhood were both spiritual and corporal. In the latter category they were to give food to the hungry, drink to the thirsty, clothing to the naked and shelter to the weary. They were to visit the sick or imprisoned, ransom captives and bury the dead. Funds for carrying out these deeds and for the building of hospitals and churches came almost entirely from private donations and legacies. It was essentially a Portuguese organisation with centres all over Portugal and it spread all over the world wherever the Portuguese settled. It continues its charitable work among the young and the old to this day.

The narrow street on the left of the Tavira Misericórdia Church soon reaches the highest and oldest part of the town: a hilltop once occupied by a Moorish fort and a mosque which were replaced in the mid-13th century by a Portuguese castle and a Christian church. The castle, small with well-tended gardens, is worth visiting for the view from its turrets over elegant Pombaline rooftops out to the abandoned tuna factories and the coastline.

Tavira riverfront.

Right: Tavira rooftops.

The Santa Maria do Castelo church next to the castle replaced a mosque on the same spot very soon after the expulsion of the Moors. It is said that during a period of truce, Muslims treacherously killed seven knights who were out hunting. The Christian reaction to this was particularly appalling even by medieval standards. Near to the tomb of the conqueror, Correia, by the chancel of the church, are the tombs of the slain seven. Although very much restored, the church contains a few interesting Gothic features, 18th-century tile murals and some unusual carvings and paintings. Of the rest of Tavira's churches, the one to see is the Carmo church on the other side of the river. Plain outside, it is a scene of baroque fantasia within.

Back on the west side, Tavira's extensive salt pans are situated along the palm lined riverside road, past the bandstand and the market, beyond the derelict cannery buildings and hulks of wooden boats. Salt has been produced here in quantity for at least 2,000 years. The production process has not changed. It is based on the fact that seawater contains three per cent salt and that the Algarve has long hot summers. The seawater is allowed to flow into evaporation pans, each as big as a football field. In the first pans, suspended impurities such as sand drop to the bottom. Clear and concentrated salt water passes to crystallising pans where the last of the water evaporates and the salt is deposited like slush. It is raked into rows and allowed to drain before being lifted out of the pans for final drying in huge heaps. Only the best quality salt is used for the table. The rest has many domestic and industrial uses: for preserving fish, curing hides and in the manufacture of glass, enamel, washing powder, baking soda, bleach, chlorine and other everyday products. The pans, incidentally, make good feeding grounds for wading birds. One of the most typical is the black-winged stilt. As its name suggests, it is a striking black and white bird with very long, red legs.

Small boat sailors and windsurfers have the choice of the open sea or sheltered lagoon waters.

You have to take the road through the salt pans to get to the nearest beaches. The 2 km road ends at a little wharf where ferry boats ply to and from the long sandbar known as the Ilha de Tavira, an excellent stretch of

Octopus, regarded locally as a gastronomic delight, is caught in pots, then hung out to dry.

Above: Tavira spare ribs and Santa Luzia pot-pourri.

beach for windsurfing. The island beach can also be reached by miniature railway from Pedras d'el Rei on the west side of Santa Luzia.

Santa Luzia

At Santa Luzia and Olhão, more than anywhere else in the Algarve, men play a metal ball bowling game called "malha."

Legend has it that the village of Santa Luzia, on the edge of the lagoon in the lee of Ilha de Tavira, was given its un-Portuguese sounding name after an effigy of the Virgin Mary was washed ashore from an Italian vessel which foundered nearby in ancient times. Evidence of what makes the village tick nowadays is strewn in piles all along the waterfront - earthenware pots, all of them numbered, some of them looking as if they have spent a lot of time in the sea. They are octopus pots. The fishermen here have long specialised in catching octopus just off the coasts of the eastern Algarve and south-western Andalusia. They lay out hundreds of pots at a time, leaving them unbaited on the sea floor in shallow water. Octopuses are attracted into them simply because of their love for lurking in holes and crevices. When the octopus boats come in, usually in the afternoon, a siren heralds the start of the daily auction on the wharf. The older fishermen remember when a boat could bring in 40 or 50 cases, each containing 40 kilos of octopus, most of which was exported to Japan. These days they are lucky to bring in half a dozen cases which are mostly sent to Lisbon and Oporto.

There are two main ways of preparing and cooking octopus. Small specimens do not need any tenderising, but the fishermen beat the larger ones against the rocks. A mallet in the kitchen has the same effect. They are then boiled thoroughly in a pressure cooker before being stripped of their skin. The other way is to hang the octopus up to dry out thoroughly, then charcoal grill and serve as small chewy pieces. This goes down well particularly with the macho types. The smell of grilling octopus is one of the most characteristic odours of Algarve fairs and festivals. The firm, spicy taste is much enjoyed in Portugal, along the Mediterranean and in the Far East, but few people in northern Europe care for it. Not to despair. There are plenty of other seafoods available and there is no better place to find them than in Olhão, the Algarve's number one fishing port.

Olhão

*T*he only thing worth pausing to look at on the N125 between Tavira and Olhão is the church at Luz de Tavira with its huge renaissance front doorway and Manueline side door. The main chapel inside has Moorish-style paving tiles made in Seville in the 15th century. Oddly, there is nothing nearly so old as this in Olhão even though a whole section of Olhão is positively Moorish-looking. In fact, the Moors had long gone by the time Olhão was anything more than a few fishermen's shacks. It was only in the early 18th century that the present town began to take shape. The old quarter is like a *medina* transplanted from North Africa with its cube-shaped, flat roofed houses separated only by narrow alleyways of cobbles. The only explanation you hear for its arabesque appearance is that Olhão traders were architecturally influenced by frequent visits to Morocco. After all, Olhão is closer by sea to Tangier than to Lisbon.

To get to the heart of Olhão, ignore the depressing apartment blocks in the front part of the town and go straight to the port or the waterfront markets. The port, on the east side, harbours a multitude of fishing

The parish church at the village of Luz de Tavira, a fine example of renaissance architecture beside the N125.

vessels from deep sea trawlers and sardine boats, to the small, brightly coloured boats that work the inshore waters with eyes painted on their bows to let the sea god know they are under the protection of the more powerful sun god. While most of the seafood landed at Olhão is destined for other parts of the country and abroad, an amazing assortment goes straight to the fish market on the Avenida 5 de Outubro, Olhão's waterfront boulevard. It is housed in one of a pair of slightly bizarre, brick buildings complete with silver domes on each corner.

Fish varieties

Prawns are probably less expensive in Olhão than anywhere in the Algarve, but nowhere are they really cheap anymore.

*T*he variety of fish and shellfish available every morning, except Sundays, in this and every other large market in the Algarve is surprisingly large compared with the very limited range on offer on most restaurant menus. Swordfish appears on Portuguese menus as *peixe espadarte*. It is one of the world's most sought after game fish with a near-white, firm, close grained flesh. It is served as steaks, usually grilled. In Spain, swordfish is called *peixe espada* and this sometimes gives rise to confusion here. *Peixe espada* in Portugal is scabbard fish, a totally different species. It is a long, narrow fish, silver and perfectly smooth skinned. In the market they will automatically slice it into sections for ease of carrying. It must be eaten same-day fresh otherwise the flesh goes pulpy. It is best dipped in flour and fried crispy. Small red mullet (*salmonete*) are also good crispy fried, the larger ones are best grilled. The Portuguese rate red mullet highly, but a lot of people can't be bothered with the small bones of which there are a great many. Bream (*besugo*) is a very bony fish which is usually served in restaurants with head and all, but it is juicy, never dry. Bass (*robalo*) is served as steaks or cooked whole in the oven with potatoes and onions. Hotel restaurants tend to buy up most of the available bass. You can also buy it fresh in beach bars with good contacts among local rod and line fishermen.

The availability of tuna (*atum*) is very seasonal. It is most readily available and of best quality during spring and early summer. Easily identified by its dark flesh, the texture and flavour of tuna is the nearest fish comes to red meat. If it is on the menu, ask whether it is fresh or frozen. A fresh tuna steak served with onions is delicious, but freezing can make it unappetisingly dry. Brill (*cherne*) is a prized fish in Portugal. The Portuguese are particularly partial to the very large head (*cabeça de cherne*) and are adept at picking their way through its mass of bones and gills. Otherwise, cherne is served as steaks. Hake (*pescada*) is much more highly rated here than in Britain. The big ones are served as cutlets, grilled or boiled. The small ones (*pescadinhas*) are fried and presented tail-in -mouth. Smelt (*carapau*) are often confused with sardines, but they are scaleless and much more expensive. The bony ridge on their sides should be cut out before frying, though this is not necessary if they

Municipal fish markets sell all kinds of freshly caught seafood each morning from Tuesday to Saturday. Supplies are limited on Monday mornings because Sunday is a day of rest for most fishermen. The market in Faro is the only one in the Algarve selling fresh fish on Sunday mornings.

133

Shallow eastern shores.
Photo: Parque Natural da Ria Formosa.

are to be grilled whole and ungutted like sardines. All these types of fish and many more are landed at Olhão along with cockles, mussels, cuttlefish, crabs, squid, octopus, shrimps, prawns, crayfish and lobster. You can have a seafood meal anywhere along the Algarve coast, but nowhere will you find one fresher or cheaper than in the restaurants along the narrow, cobbled streets in the old quarter of Olhão opposite the market.

Places of interest to visit in the vicinity of Olhão include Moncarapacho where the Church of Santo Cristo has an impressive late 16th-century altar-piece and 17th-century polychromatic tiles. The small, local museum is next to it. The Grotto of Moncarapacho is a short drive away atop a hill called Cerro da Cabeça and there is a belvedere lookout at the 410m summit of the nearby Monte de São Miguel. Fuseta, 8 km back along the coast from Olhão, has the ruins of a small castle and it shares Olhão's fascination for cubic houses with roof terraces. The chimneys of Fuseta are also like those of Olhão but different to all the others in the Algarve. Instead of being prominent with intricate patterns, the "balloon chimneys" of Fuseta and Olhão are of a simple, square design and they sit low and squat.

Don't let the bustle or fishy smell of the Olhão waterfront deter you from getting on a small ferry boat bound for the fresh air and translucent waters at any of the excellent beaches on nearby islands. There are regular services to Farol, Hangares and Culatra beaches on Ilha da Culatra, and Armona and Fuseta on Ilha da Armona.

Like Faro, Olhão overlooks the Ria Formosa, a refuge not only for aquatic birds, but an aquatic dog: *cão de água* or Portuguese water dog. A breeding programme was instituted as part of the conservation work of the Ria Formosa reserve because there were fears for the future of the breed. The origins of the Portuguese water dog are not known but it is believed to be an extremely old breed. It is said to have been routinely carried on Portuguese caravels and galleons. Ironically, the oldest surviving English pet painting is a portrait of a Portuguese water dog called "Bungey" who lived in the 16th century. They are medium sized dogs, usually all black or dark brown with a curly or wavy coat, drop ears, a top knot and a curled up tail ending in a tuft. It is a sturdier looking fellow than the poodle, but what makes him different to nearly all other dogs is that his feet are webbed. This obviously helps in swimming. Portuguese water dogs are credited with the ability to dive to depths of 4m and swim underwater to steer shoals of fish into nets. More plausibly, they used to help out by retrieving drifting tackle, taking rope ends from one boat to another and guarding boats

Manueline side door of the Luz de Tavira parish church.

on the beach. Their numbers seriously dwindled at the turn of the century. Modern fishing methods made the dogs redundant. There are very few working dogs left in the Algarve, the last stronghold of the breed in Portugal. Fortunately, they make alert and energetic pets most of which are registered with a national association of breeders. Still, there may be little more than 1,000 Portuguese water dogs left in the world, mainly in the Algarve, Britain and the North America.

Portuguese water dog.

Page opposite:
Olhão barber shop.

The West Coast

From Sagres to Aljezur

The west coast of the Algarve is different because it has been left alone by the developers. It has been left alone because it is considered too far from Faro airport and because it has the reputation of being windswept and desolate. Another reason was added a few years ago: the Government declared the whole of the coastal strip from Sines, south of Lisbon, to Salema, west of Lagos, a protected zone. This was not the same as turning it into a national park or a nature reserve, but it meant that the west coast had been recognised as a place of special environmental and ecological importance which had to be conserved.

The most southerly community in Portugal and the most south-westerly in continental Europe is at Sagres. As you approach it on the road from Vila do Bispo you are travelling across typical cape terrain: flat, almost treeless and somewhat forbidding. The village of Sagres itself is a motley collection of plain buildings overlooking the Bay of Sagres which is flanked by two headlands: Atalaia Point and Sagres Point. It is only when you catch sight of the grey ramparts of the fortress blocking off the massive plateau of Sagres Point and cast your eye around the 10 km arc of sheer cliffs to the lighthouse at Cape St Vincent that you get a real feeling for the tremendous historical importance of this place. It was at least as important during the Age of Discovery as Cape Kennedy was during the early years of space exploration. When the weather is fair, it can be a powerful sensation to sit quietly anywhere along the clifftops here and look out to sea and ponder the extraordinary adventurers who have passed this way.

A place to sit and ponder...

Voyages of discovery

The first landfall west of these cliffs is the island of Santa Maria in the Azores group, 875 nautical miles away. The next is the coast of Virginia which is about 3,500 miles distant. There is no way, of course, that seafarers in the ancient world could have

138

known these simple facts of geography. To the Phoenicians, Greeks, Carthaginians and Romans this was both a holy and a terrifying place. The Greek author, Strabo, who lived at the time of Christ, put it more matter-of-factly in declaring that this was "not only the end of Europe, but of all the inhabited earth." Although there is some evidence in the form of Carthaginian coins that storm driven vessels may have reached the Azores as early as the 4th century BC and that Roman galleys may have been carried all the way across to the Americas, there is no evidence to suggest they ever came back to tell the tale. No one would have expected them to, for what lay out there beyond the horizon where the huge sun sank into the sea each evening was dreadful to contemplate and certainly beyond human comprehension. It was to this remote and solitary place that the Infante D. Henrique, Prince

Well known to modern seafarers, the first and last light in southern Europe.

Henry the Navigator, came in the 15th century to work on his obsession to push back the frontiers of the known world.

A few galleys manned by Genoese or Catalans from the Mediterranean may have bravely ventured far out into the Atlantic in the 13th and 14th centuries and perhaps some of them got as far as the Azores and Madeira, the latter being about 600 miles south-west of the Algarve. These were haphazard trips, sporadic and unsponsored. It was not until the 15th century that ocean travel came to be methodically planned, systematically logged and fully supported by monarchs, governments and later by merchant companies. The first sponsor and the instigator of the first epic voyages of discovery was Henry the Navigator.

While precise information about Henry is far from complete, it is clear he was a most remarkable man. He was a prince, politician, warrior and grand master of the Order of Christ, but his fame endures mainly because of his monumental contribution

The approaches to Sagres fortress by land and by sea have always been stark.

Nowadays, woollies against the wind sell well at stalls just outside the entrance to Sagres fortress. Inside, at the far end of this precipitous promontory, anglers with long rods cast from the clifftops for sea bass and bream.

to geographical discovery and the opening up of trade and cultural links between Europe and the East. When he arrived to settle in the Algarve as Governor in 1419 he was a tall, well built, blond haired young man of 25. He was austere and devoutly religious. A veteran of the invasion of Ceuta over the Straits from Gibraltar, he retained an abiding zeal to banish Muslims from North Africa and the Holy Land once and for all. While in Ceuta, where he fought with distinction in 1415, he had learned from traders about gold routes across the Sahara which were thought to originate in Guinea on the African west coast. Crusading reverence coupled with a thirst for gold revenue were soon to be augmented by an obsession to find Prester John, the legendary priest-king who ruled supreme amid fabulous wealth somewhere in Africa or the Orient. Religion and economics - God and gold - were the catalysts. Sagres was the crucible.

The exact location of Henry's so-called school of navigation is not known. It is generally accepted that while Henry's ships were built and harboured at Lagos, he sited his headquarters at Sagres and created a settlement on land granted by the crown. The settlement came to be known as Vila do Infante, or Prince's town. This is popularly believed to have been situated on the headland within the walls of the *forteleza* which were rebuilt after the 1755 earthquake. The only building still surviving and thought to have been around in more or less its present form in Henry's day, is the starkly simple little church within the fortress. Just as there is doubt about the location of Henry's headquarters, so the exact form of the school of navigation is unclear. It may have been a formal academy, or perhaps it was a looser arrangement around or within the royal court. In any case, it was like a magnet to the best brains in Europe concerned with the nautical sciences. Under Henry's patronage, they came here to teach and to study. A community of brilliant scholars accumulated and correlated nautical knowledge as it became available. They established a data bank, so to speak, which was continually added to as information was brought back by the captains of successive voyages to hitherto unknown places. The scholars in turn instructed less experienced captains about Atlantic currents and wind systems and the latest navigational methods. Cartography was refined with the use of newly devised instruments. Maps were regularly updated and extended. A revolutionary type of vessel, the caravel, was designed.

When Henry began master-minding and directing operations at Sagres and Lagos in 1419, the known southern limit of the Atlantic Ocean was the dreaded Cape Bojador in West Africa just below

The church the fortress overlooks Tonel beach.

latitude 27.N. It was dreaded in the same way Cape St Vincent had been dreaded by the ancients. Apart from all the superstitions about seething serpents and monsters, the northern side of the cape, which juts out into the ocean for 25 miles, is notoriously dangerous because of the violence of its waves and currents, and the treacherous nature of its shallows and frequent mists. It was known to Arab geographers as "the Green Sea of Darkness." Furthermore, the prevailing winds are northerlies and ships of the time had extreme difficulty in sailing against the wind. All this fuelled the deep-seated belief that if you rounded the cape, there was no possibility of return. Cape Bojador, therefore, was not only a dreadful physical barrier but a terrible psychological one. Many attempts failed before the barrier was finally overcome by the Portuguese in 1434. The first European captain to round Cape Bojador was Gil Eanes, of Lagos. His heroic feat represented perhaps the greatest achievement of Henry's lifetime. This and subsequent heroic voyages probing farther and farther down the African west coast were made possible by Lagos-built caravels.

For many hundreds of years the vessels which plied the waters off the Algarve were of two basic types: oar-propelled galleys some of which carried a sail, or bulkier, more ponderous, square-sailed merchantmen. At the beginning of the 15th century, sailing ships still had only one mast and one sail. The caravel made such vessels obsolete. As devised by Henry's experts, the caravel was a broad-beamed craft of about 50 or 60 tons and about 25 metres in length. It was built of flush-fitted planks attached to a previously assembled frame. Usually it had a double tower at the stern, the sterncastle, and a single tower in the bow forming the forecastle. It had two or three pole masts and was lateen-rigged. Its triangular sails were set on long yards which sloped down from well above the mast almost to deck level. This type of rigging, which the Portuguese almost certainly adapted from Arab versions, was carried so that the sails received the wind on either side, keeping the same edge forward unlike square-riggers. Over the years, the design of caravels

Page opposite:
West Coast farmlands,
where traditional
methods linger, are
devoted mostly to the
growing of grain crops.

Henry's portrait hangs
in the pousada at Sagres.

At Martinhal there are
remnants of kilns which
produced amphorae
used for conveying
goods in Roman galleys.

underwent modification and later models featured a fourth mast which carried a square sail for running before the wind. Lightness and speed were two of the caravel's strong points, but most outstanding of all was its capacity for sailing to windward. It was this capacity, unique in its day, that allowed Portugal's 15th-century heroes to sail beyond all known limits and return to tell of their experiences. The advantages of the caravel over previous designs was quickly recognised and copied, first by the Spanish and then by every maritime country in Europe. In the second half of the 15th century, it was caravels which carried Portuguese discoverers, traders and colonisers beyond the equator and eventually beyond the Cape of Good Hope into the Indian Ocean.

Henry lived in the vicinity of Sagres for most of his life and this is where he died on November 13, 1460 at the age of 66. He had opened the way, but had not lived long enough to savour and share the successes of Bartolomeu Dias who rounded the Cape of Good Hope in 1488, and Vasco da Gama who finally pushed through the sea route to India in 1498. No doubt he would have been utterly fascinated too by the exploits of that other great voyager of the late 15th century, Christopher Columbus.

According to most authorities, Columbus was born in Genoa on the north-west coast of Italy. The eldest of five children, he was not yet nine years old at the time of Henry's death. There seemed no likelihood that the life's work of the two men would be similar in any way. With little formal education, young Christopher followed in the footsteps of his father and maternal grandfather and was trained in the wool weaving trade. Genoa was a leading port and Christopher made several short trips to sea while still a teenager. By his early twenties he had sailed as far as the Aegean. He was 24 years old when by one of those quirks of fate he ended up on the doorstep of the Sagres school of navigation. He was with an armed convoy on its way from Genoa to England in May 1476 when it was attacked by pirates off Cape St Vincent. His ship went down in the ensuing fight and, though wounded, he managed to escape by swimming six miles to shore.

How long he spent in the Algarve is not known. He is said to have spent some time recuperating in Lisbon, a city he came to know well. In 1478 he sailed from Lisbon to Portuguese Madeira as a buying agent for a major Genoese company. The following year he married the daughter of the governor of the island of Porto Santo in the Madeira group. That was where their only child, a son, was born. It was only after sailing to the Portuguese trading post of São Jorge da Mina on the Gold Coast of West Africa that Columbus got a real taste for exploration as opposed to mere business travel. It was then that the notion of voyaging westward to find new lands took hold of him and became all consuming.

Though they came from totally different backgrounds, Columbus and Henry the Navigator had much in common. They were both devoutly religious. In the words of Ferdinand, his scholarly second son, born illegitimately to his Spanish mistress after the death of his wife, Columbus "was so strict in matters of religion he might have been taken for a member of a religious order." Columbus, like Henry, was able to reconcile his extreme Christian fervour

Page opposite:
Prince Henry is known to have regularly worshipped at the Chapel of Nossa Senhora de Guadaloupe, near Raposeira, one of the oldest chapels in the Algarve. The Chapel of Santa Catarina at Beliche (bottom) came later. It was originally built in 1632 and rebuilt after the 1755 earthquake.

Beliche beach.

a scientifically enquiring mind and the quest for worldly riches. They both set about their various projects with formidable courage, dedication and tenacity. However, in at least one respect they were totally at odds: Henry was convinced that the way to reach the East was to go south; Columbus believed the best route lay to the west. Columbus first submitted his plan to sail west to the Orient to the King of Portugal. A maritime committee appointed by King João II considered the proposals but rejected them on the grounds that Columbus's calculations were wrong. Only after this rejection and after the death of his wife, Dona Filipa, did Columbus leave his adopted country with his legitimate son, Diego, to seek sponsorship for his proposals from King Ferdinand and Queen Isabella of Spain. A deal was agreed after seven years of wrangling. And thus it was under the Spanish rather than the Portuguese flag that he discovered the New World.

Shops haven't changed much in West Coast villages and there are few of them.

The above is a brief summary of conventional wisdom on the subject, parts of which at least were hotly disputed by some authorities in the rash of

books on Columbus published to mark the 500th anniversary of his 1492 voyage to America. Lisbon University historian, Mascarenhas Barreto, argues in his book *The Portuguese Columbus: Secret Agent of King John II*, published by Macmillan Press, that the great man was in fact a Portuguese spy in the court of the Spanish monarchs. Spain, of course, was Portugal's arch rival in the discovery stakes and it is claimed that Columbus' job was to lead the Spanish monarchs astray by probing westward to try and find India while his Portuguese compatriots headed in the right direction.

*C*olumbus's introduction to Portugal back in 1476 was probably not the first and certainly not the last skirmish involving famous men off the Sagres and Cape St Vincent headlands. That old sea dog Sir Francis Drake was very active in these waters harrying Spanish galleons returning from the Caribbean laden with treasure to fill Spain's war chest. Portugal was under Spanish rule at the time. With preparations well advanced for the "invincible armada" to invade England in 1587, Drake was sent by Elizabeth I to "singe the King of Spain's beard" in Cadiz harbour 150 miles east of Sagres. After destroying Spanish ships as they lay at anchor in Cadiz and captured a great cargo vessel loaded with spices from the East, he went on to raze Vila do Infante. It was the year before the doomed Spanish armada set sail from Lisbon.

Admiral Tourville with a French fleet of 71 warships defeated a British fleet commanded by Sir George Rooke off Cape St Vincent in 1693, and the English admiral Sir George Rodney defeated the Spanish admiral Don Juan de Langara here while on his way to relieve Gibraltar in 1790. In 1833, Admiral Sir Charles Napier on behalf of Queen Maria II of Portugal engaged a naval squadron supporting her usurper uncle, Miguel. The English admiral had 176 guns against the Miguelites' 372. Manoeuvring in a light breeze, Napier's 46-gun frigate *Rainha* crippled two 86-gun Miguelite men-of-war. The rest of the Miguelite squadron was captured and that effectively sewed up

Sea battles

Troubled waters....

Portugal's War of the Two Brothers. Perhaps Napier had taken inspiration from a previous engagement, the most famous of them all, which is named after the cape.

The Battle of Cape St Vincent took place on February 14, 1797 between a Spanish fleet under the command of Don José de Cordoba and a British fleet under Sir John Jervis. Spain at the time was a pawn of France in the latter's hostilities with England, just as Portugal had been a pawn of Spain two centuries earlier. The Spanish fleet consisted of 27 ships-of-the-line in a state of neglect. They had been forced to put to sea hastily manned by soldiers and press-ganged landlubbers. The fleet was drifting in disarray about 25 miles south-west of the cape when Sir John arrived on the scene from Lisbon with 15 ships-of-the-line.

He attacked the Spaniards without hesitation having ordered his ships into a single line ahead formation. Jervis adopted this formation because he had seen that the disorganised Spanish fleet was in two sections: six of their ships had separated from the main body and thus formed a vulnerable unit.   The British sailed through the gap between the two sections. To leeward, the six isolated Spaniards sheered off and disengaged in the face of rapid and accurate fire from the British, though one of them managed to cross astern of the British line and rejoin the main group. Having sailed through the gap, the plan was for the British ships to

attack in succession to meet the windward position of the enemy. The commander of the *Captain*, third from the end of the line, realised that if all the British ships completed the manoeuvre, the Spaniards might be able to avoid further engagement by steering to the north. To thwart their escape, he acted without orders and broke from the line to put himself across the bows of the Spaniards. On seeing what had happened, Jervis approved the initiative of the *Captain* and ordered his other ships in the rear to break off. The Spanish commanders with their hopelessly inept crews were unable to effectively respond. Even their flagship, the huge 112-gun *Santissima Trinidad* seemed helpless when set upon by the *Captain* whose crew went on to further distinguish themselves by boarding and capturing the 112-gun *San Josef* and the 80-gun *San Nicolas*. After two other Spanish ships surrendered, Jervis ordered a stop to the engagement and allowed the *Santissima Trinidad* and the others to retreat to Cadiz. Sir John Jervis became Earl St Vincent and was granted a pension of £3,000. He went on to become Admiral of the Fleet. The young commander of the *Captain* who had shown such excellent judgement, courage and initiative was made a Knight of the Bath and promoted to the rank of rear-admiral within days of this important victory. The Battle of Cape St Vincent had brought to the attention of the British public for the first time a brilliant new national hero. His name was Horatio Nelson.

It was near here that the young man who was to become Britain's greatest naval hero out-gunned the Spanish.

Nelson was very familiar with the imposing sight of Cape St Vincent and Sagres Point having passed this way many times, the last being in September 1805 on his way to Cadiz and then on to Trafalgar. The scene has not changed much since then. He would still recognise the grim Sagres fortress and the much smaller Fort de Beliche perched on the much indented cliffs just short of Cape St Vincent. The lower buildings on the tip of Cape St Vincent itself might seem familiar but what would be starkly different is the lighthouse tower above them. Cape St Vincent lighthouse was built on the site of a 16th-century Franciscan convent in 1846. It was electrified in 1906. It is situated at the end of the 6 km road from Sagres. There is plenty of parking and visitors are welcome to walk around the lighthouse grounds and climb the 73-step tower. Your guide will be one of the lighthouse keepers who will explain that the two 3,000-watt lamps magnified by concentric rows of prisms throw a 10 foot tall beam 100 miles out to sea making it the second most powerful lighthouse in Europe. It keeps vigil over one of the world's busiest shipping lanes. All shipping from and through the Mediterranean to the west coast of Europe and most of the eastern seaboard of North America passes this way.

Cape St Vincent's flora and fauna

Pimpernels are sometimes scarlet, but most often in the Algarve they are blue and to be found among rock crevices and sand dunes.

At first glance, the cliff tops between Sagres and Cape St Vincent seem stony and arid and vegetated only by prickly scrub, but closer examination in spring will reveal an extraordinarily rich flora, including species found nowhere else in the world. At least three are named after the cape: *Scilla vincentina, Centaurea vincentia* and *Biscutella vincentia*. Tiny crevices and shallow depressions with almost no soil

manage to support vivid blue shrubby pimpernel (*Anagallis monelli*), tiny yellow hoop-petticoat daffodils (*Narcissus bolbocodium*) and clumps of thrift (*Armeria pungens*). At the end of summer when all the other wildflowers have withered, white sea daffodils (*Pabcratium maritimum*) stage a colourful finale. It will not be long before the show starts again in early spring with *Asteriscus maritimus* daisies. This is rich hunting ground indeed for the botanist.

You do not need to be an ornithologist or an experienced birdwatcher to appreciate the bird life in this area. In spring and autumn, the headlands offer an ideal vantage point from which to observe seabird migration. With patience and a keen eye you may be fortunate enough to see huge numbers of seabirds in passage between the Mediterranean and north-western Europe flying northwards towards their breeding grounds in January, February and March, southward to their winter haunts in September, October and November. The most easily recognisable and the most spectacular to watch in passage is the gannet. Gannets are large, oceanic birds with snowy white plumage and extensive black wingtips. Immature birds are dusky brown all over in their first year, mottled pied in their second and third years. Their flight is quite different from gulls, which in any case are smaller. When looking for food, gannets wheel in the air or beat upwind on stiff wings with their beaks pointing down. On spotting a fish, they go into a slanting or vertical dive with their wings angled back. On their way down, they adjust their position minutely by moving their wingtips, rotating their bodies slightly, using their tails as a rudder and their feet as flaps. They plunge like a torpedo into the water directly on top of their target sending up a plume of spray. By the time they surface a few second later and take off again, they have already swallowed their prey, usually a large mackerel or herring. While in passage but not hunting for food, their flight pattern is quite different. Then they generally skim fairly close to the surface with a flapping flight interspersed with glides. The line of flight is direct and purposeful.

Birds travelling over long distances have no need to rely on navigational aids such as the 1,000 watt lamp at Cape St Vincent which when magnified through prisms throws a beam up to 90 km out to sea.

Two-thirds of the world's gannets breed on 14 gannetries around the British Isles, most notably on St Kilda in the Outer Hebrides and on Bass Rock in the Firth of Forth. As soon as the chicks are ready to leave the cliff ledges and fend for themselves, the crowded, raucous colonies split up and the breeding cliffs are deserted. Juvenile birds set off for more bountiful fishing grounds as far away as the equatorial waters of west Africa. Adult gannets rarely travel so far. Large numbers of juveniles, young adults and fully mature birds favour the Mediterranean and the waters off the Algarve's south coast. In September, October and November they make their way down Portugal's west coast, travelling singly, in pairs or more usually in small squadrons. Their flight lines are exactly parallel to the shipping lanes. Anyone fortunate enough to be watching at the right time as gannets are rounding the Cape St Vincent and Sagres headlands will be given a rare insight into just how precisely birds are able to navigate during long-distance migration. Having flown more than 1,500 miles (2,400 km) from their breeding grounds, passing many rocky headlands on the way, gannets arrive a few hundred metres out to

Gannets fishing.

sea off Cape St Vincent. Instead of carrying straight on in the direction of Casablanca in Morocco, they turn and put themselves in line to pass a few hundred metres off the Sagres point. Once there, they turn again. They are now flying a course roughly parallel to the Algarve south coast. As they approached Cape St Vincent they were flying almost due south. As they leave the Sagres headland they are flying almost due east. They move through this 90 degree change of course without the slightest hesitation. There is no confusion, no dithering even among unaccompanied juvenile birds which have never passed this way before.

On good days, gannets pass within normal eyesight range at a rate of many hundreds an hour. Sandwich terns, though never in such large numbers, hug the shore more closely. Puffins and razorbills as well as cory and Balaeric shearwaters pass much farther out and are generally only seen with the aid of binoculars. Experienced birdwatchers may spot the occasional pomarine and arctic skua. Farther out still, on the edge of the Continental Shelf a couple of hours' boat ride away, Wilson's petrels and sooty shearwaters pass on their round-the-world wanderings from the Antarctic and the islands of the southern oceans. They circumnavigate the world with an apparent ease which would have truly astounded Henry the Navigator.

The most characteristic land birds of the Cape are black redstarts, spotless starlings, blue rock thrushes, rock doves, jackdaws and the odd breeding pair of peregrine falcons. Alpine accentors are unusual visitors which move about the cliff scree in winter. Choughs congregate in winter and disperse again in spring to breed on the west coast cliffs. It is possible you will catch sight of the chough's larger cousin, the raven. There was a time, according to legend, when you could not fail to have seen at least 10 ravens.

The Cape is at its most awesome on wild , wintery days, but to observe its flora and fauna it is best visited on mild, clear days in spring.

The Cape takes its name from a Spanish priest martyred at the beginning of the 4th century, whose remains were brought or washed ashore on Promontorium Sacrum, the Sacred Cape, as it was known in ancient times. A temple is said to have been built where Vincent's remains were buried. The temple, perhaps on the site of the Forte de Beliche, was watched over by 10 ravens which never left it. During the reign of Afonso Henriques (1139 - 85), Vincent's remains were exhumed and taken by ship for reburial in Lisbon to protect them from desecration by the Muslims. The ravens, according to legend, kept constant vigil from the rigging of the ship all the way. Because of this the raven is still part of the insignia of both the city of Lisbon and of Cape St Vincent's local seat of administration, Vila do Bispo.

The mystique as well as the physical grandeur of Sagres and Cape St Vincent attract great numbers of day-trippers. Those who choose to stay a few days, or even weeks, can do so in style at the Pousada Infante, or more modestly at all sorts of lesser accommodation down to cheap, private rooms and a friendly camp site.

Hitch-hiking in the Algarve is not always easy...

Those who arrive to stay a while are usually glad to be at the end of the line, on the outer fringe of Algarve tourism, away from the glitz of the commercial south coast. A great many arrive with packs on their backs and with Australian, New Zealand, American, Canadian or South African accents. The square in front of the Café Conchina is the main meeting place for back-packers by day. It is the point of arrival and departure for buses, the junction between boarding house and beach, a place to linger and meet new friends over coffee or beer. In the evening, the scene shifts slightly to inexpensive restaurants and watering holes with names like the Quatro dos Ventos and the Last Chance.

There are four good beaches in the neighbourhood. Praia do Martinhal is the farthest from the village, but it is the biggest and the most protected if a westerly wind is blowing. It stretches from the Baleeira fishing harbour to an outcrop of low cliffs, the site of a Roman settlement which specialised in the production of amphorae. Praia da Mareta just below the village and facing south-east is tucked in the lee of Sagres Point. Over on the other side and facing west is Tonel, a small beach with steep access. There is a long beach at Beliche. It is perhaps the best around Sagres so long as a strong westerly is not blowing.

The beaches up the west coast are fantastic, many of them comprising of acres of nearly deserted sand backed by dunes or cliffs looking out over lines of surf cascading in on the wildly beautiful shore. Among the most breathtaking are the ones on either side of a loop road - more of a track really - which runs along the clifftops adjacent to the old village of Carrapateira, 14 km north of Vila do Bispo. Apart from a couple of beach bars, the coastline here is total natural. There are a few rooms to be had near the village a kilometre or so back from the sea.

The next communities of any size on the seaward side of the main road running north are an unfinished development, A Telha Velha, near the fishing village of Arrifana, and a holiday fishermen's shanty town next to the big beach at Monte Clérico. Moving north, the next unspoilt beach (it has a camp site not far away) is

West coast boarding-houses are modest, but the beaches are breath-taking.

at Amoreira which can be reached by turn-offs after the main west coast town of Aljezur. It is a town worth pausing to take a look at.

Aljezur

*A*ljezur sits on either side of a broad river valley through which only a stream trickles nowadays. The whole town is presided over by the ruins of a hilltop castle on the most defensible spot in the area. The castle was captured from the Moors in 1249 by Dom Paio Peres Correira, the most famous Portuguese commander during the reconquest of the Algarve outside of royalty. He was master of the Knights of Santiago, one of the strongest orders of chivalry in southern Portugal in the 13th century. The story goes that Peres Correira's troops took the castle without a fight one night after a Muslim maiden opened the doors and let them in. Legend has it that the defending soldiers were all down at the beach having a midnight swim at the time.

Drive or climb up the steep streets for a fine view over the town and surrounding countryside. From here

'new' Aljezur from the castle.

the town can be seen to consist of two parts. The old part hugs the hillside while the "new" part is on the far side of the fertile valley which takes on a colourful patchwork appearance when the crops are growing. The old parish church dates from the 14th century though it has been much rebuilt. The "new" church across the way was built in the 18th century and was intended to be the nucleus of a remodelled town. The man behind this project was Dom Francisco Gomes, Bishop of Faro. He wanted to encourage the townsfolk to move away from the river at the base of the old quarter because it was a notorious breeding ground for mosquitoes which in those days carried malaria and were the cause of frequent epidemics. As can be seen, the Bishop was only partly heeded. Fever or no fever, many of the people of Aljezur decided to stay put on the west side. The most likely ailment one is likely to contract around here nowadays is a headache from too much sun or too much wine. In the church on the "new" side of town you will find the skulls of the last two Moors to be killed in Aljezur. It has long been a local belief that if you lay your hand on one of the skulls, your headache will go away.

Beyond Aljezur the countryside is more sparsely populated and the beaches are even less frequented. There are beaches hidden away at the end of long tracks from the peanut growing area of Rogil, but there is also a much more easily accessible and popular beach at the river mouth 4 km west of the village of Odeceixe. As at Amoreira, the beach at Odeceixe offers the choice of bathing in the river or in the sea. The Odeceixe river cuts right across the beach and forms the boundary between the Algarve and the next province of Alentejo. The boundary moves every year as the river's course alters with the shifting sands. This shifts responsibilities for cleaning and generally administering the beach. In a country which revels in red tape, a moving provincial border must be an added delight for licence-issuing local bureaucrats.

Inland Algarve

From the Atlantic to the Guadiana

For a glimpse of what "normal" life in the Algarve is like, it is best to visit the towns, villages and countryside inland. They have remained mostly untouched by tourism and large-scale development. There are no crowds of south coast holidaymakers, but nor is there the desolation of the west coast. The life-style is unsophisticated, based on traditional values and old-fashioned ways of doing things. It is a simple life-style of a kind which is fast fading and already rare in most of modern Europe. Several north-south roads connect the south coastal strip with the hinterland and there are a few lateral roads running more or less east-west linking the inland towns and main villages. Besides these narrow but reasonably good tarred roads, there is a network of unsurfaced, rural roads. A trans-Algarve motorway, the Via do Infante, is under construction. The first section, from Estói to the Spanish border was opened in 1992. It will be extended to near Guia in 1993. On inland routes, travel by car has its obvious advantages. Although the distances involved are not great, travel by bus or hitch-hiking is only practical for those with plenty of time. Bus services are not frequent and the ease of getting lifts is unpredictable. With plenty of energy and suitable bikes, cycling is an enjoyable way of getting around most of the tarred inland roads except for the steep climb up to and beyond Monchique

The Serra de Monchique range takes its name from the small, serene town 25 km north of Portimão at the heart of a rolling expanse of heavily timbered, sporadically farmed hills. The town itself is worth a visit if only for the marvellous countryside you pass through to get there. One way to approach Monchique is from the signposted Casais turn-off nearly opposite the Hotel Penina west of Portimão. Archaeology enthusiasts will want to stop 4.5 km along this road and walk to the Neolithic dolmens, plentiful enough in Portugal, though not the Algarve. Otherwise, follow the

*January and February
is almond blossom time.
Below: Odelouca river.*

tarred road and the signs to Carrical through land used for small-scale mixed farming. You will notice the aerials atop Fóia, the Algarve's highest peak, as you begin to climb into the foothills where pine and cork oak trees and *arbutus* bushes soon give way to eucalyptus plantations.

*A*t the hamlet of Casais the choice is left to Marmalete and on to Aljezur and the west coast, or right to Monchique. The road between Aljezur and Marmalete has fairly recently been transformed from a rough, winding track into a good, surfaced road with little traffic, which slices through the forest at the northern end of the Serra Espinhaço de Cão (Dog's Back Ridge). A long, lonely, forestry track still runs down through the Espinhaço de Cão past the Bravura reservoir to link the modest village of Marmalete with the Bensafrim - Alfambra road. The Marmalete - Casais road joins the main Portimão - Monchique road at a quarry where massive blocks of granite are extracted, cut and crushed by equally massive machinery. This is the only scar on the main road stretch from Porto de Lagos to Monchique which looks its best in February and March when it is ablaze with mimosa blossom. Below this intersection, 6 km short of Monchique, the leafy little spa of Caldas de Monchique nestles at the head of a lush ravine. People have been coming here for 2,000 years to take the waters which emerge from the ground smelling slightly of sulphur at a temperature of 32° C (91°F). Roman noblemen flocked here to cure various ills, but the waters unfortunately did nothing to help the most celebrated of all visitors to the spa, João II, who suffered from dropsy. Despite prolonged treatment at Caldas de Monchique, the "Perfect Prince" died of his ailment in 1495, just two years short of realising his greatest dream - the discovery of the sea route to India. Today the whole spa is a state-run operation and its therapy clinic, open June to mid-November, offers treatment to both in and out-patients suffering from respiratory, intestinal, circulatory or muscular problems. Visitors from all over Portugal and abroad come to seek relief from asthma, rheumatism,

Caldas de Monchique

A leafy walk at Caldas.

Page opposite:
(above) near Alcalar on the road to Casais.
(below) a leafy lane in autumn near Monchique.

163

back pains and other disorders. Apart from its therapeutic properties, the spring water here is exploited commercially as table mineral water which is bottled in a modern plant at Caldas and distributed to supermarkets throughout the Algarve. Spring and early summer are the best times to drop by, for it is then that everything is in bloom and the song of Nightingales fills the thickets which provide the serene setting for Caldas' lingering hint of Victorian grandeur.

Monchique

*A*t the end of the steep 6 km section of road after Caldas, Monchique itself may come as an anti-climax. Many visitors find it so because they don't really see the town at all. They miss it by swinging around the square in front of the town and heading straight up to Fóia. Instead, it is a good idea to pause here. Park in or near the square and walk up through the narrow, cobbled streets to get the feel of how the mountain folk live. It is all rather basic, but it is also a most restful release from the real world. You can still have a pair of shoes or boots made to measure in Monchique, and if you ask around you will soon locate a bottle of moonshine *medronho* , the finest available anywhere. Bring an empty litre bottle to put it in. The parish church is remarkable for its Manueline doorway featuring a twisted rope motif. The Restaurant Central at number 5 Rua da Igreja is remarkable too. Leaving little room for its few tables and chairs, it is crammed with countless thousands of business cards, letters, messages and assorted scribblings left by decades of visitors. A steep walk up out of the town leads to another oddity - the ruins of a 1632 Franciscan convent with the neighbourhood's best view of Monchique and its wooded setting. A local farmer annexed the main altar with wire netting for his chickens and turned the sacristy into a cowshed, but even they have now moved out.

An abandoned Franciscan convent overlooks Monchique.

The steep road up to Fóia has become well-known for its piri-piri chicken restaurants. It is often shrouded in cloud during winter, but the main attraction in the warmer, drier months is the cool, clean air and the tremendous views. Above the tree-line just below the

Caldas de Monchique.

900-metre summit there are roadside spots where you can look down on a coastal panorama, albeit sometimes a misty one, stretching through 180 degrees from Odeceixe in the north-west corner of the province, all the way over to the beach which sweeps towards Vilamoura on the far side of Albufeira. You used to be able to stroll over the heathland around the obelisk on the summit, but is has now been fenced off by the military for NATO use. Before the end of the Cold War, a formidable, electronic eaves-dropping bunker joined the forest of telecommunications towers and aerials atop Fóia, presumably to track Warsaw Pact shipping around Cape St Vincent.

Atop Fóia.

Military treaties

Portugal is a founder member of NATO, but this is an infant alliance compared with the formal military agreements between Portugal and one of NATO's other founders - Britain. Portugal and Britain have been allies for an astonishingly long time - more than 600 years. Ancient treaties were evoked during secret, World War II negotiations which concluded in October 1943 with neutral Portugal agreeing to the use of the Azores by British and United States flotillas and air forces. Prior to "Operation Alacrity," German U-boats caused havoc among cross Atlantic shipping. Facilities in the Azores, including use of the aerodrome at Lajes on the island of Terceira which had the largest runway in the world at that time, meant that maritime air patrols could check the U-boat menace and make an important contribution to final victory in the Battle of the Atlantic. This agreement on use of the Azores was announced by Prime Minister Winston Churchill in the House of Commons on October 12, 1943. He emphasised that the agreement arose out of the treaty signed between Britain and Portugal in the year 1373 by King Edward III and King Ferdinand. Churchill later wrote of his announcement:

"I spoke in a level voice and made a pause to allow the House to take in the date, 1373. As this soaked in there was something like a gasp. I do not suppose any such continuity of relations between two Powers has ever been, or ever will be, set forth in the ordinary day-to-day work of British Diplomacy.

"This treaty, I went on, was reinforced in various forms by treaties of 1386, 1643, 1654, 1660, 1661, 1703 and 1815, and in a secret declaration of 1899. In more modern times the validity of the Old Treaties was recognised in the Treaties of Arbitration concluded with Portugal in 1904, and in 1914. Article I of the treaty of 1373 runs as follows :

" 'In the first place we settle and covenant that there shall be from this day forward..... true, faithful, constant, mutual and perpetual friendships, union, alliances, and deeds of sincere affection, and that as true and faithful friends we shall henceforth, reciprocally, be friends to friends and enemies to enemies, and shall assist, maintain and uphold each other mutually, by sea and by land, against all men that may live or die.'

" This engagement has lasted now for nearly six hundred years, and is without parallel in world history. I have now to announce its latest application. At the outset of war the Portuguese Government, in full agreement with His Majesty's Government in the United Kingdom, adopted a policy of neutrality with a view to preventing the war spreading into the Iberian Peninsula. The Portuguese Government have repeatedly stated, most recently in Dr Salazar's speech of April 27, that the above policy is in no way inconsistent with the Anglo-Portuguese Alliance, which was reaffirmed by

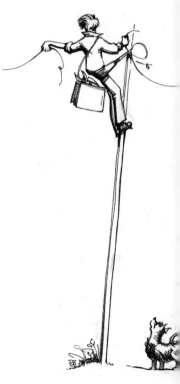

England and Portugal have kept in close touch for more than 600 years.

the Portuguese Government in the early days of the war.

His Majesty's Government of the United Kingdom basing themselves upon this ancient alliance, have now requested the Portuguese Government to accord them certain facilities in the Azores which will enable better protection to be provided for merchant shipping in the Atlantic. The Portuguese Government have agreed to grant this request, and arrangements which enter into force immediately, have been concluded between the two Governments."

Trees

While modern military and telecommunications requirements have robbed Fóia of its natural beauty, big areas of the Serra de Monchique remain relatively "unspoilt" though not untouched by farmers,

Olive trees may grow for a thousand years. The one pictured right, on the Vale da Pinta golf course, was probably around in Henry the Navigator's time.
Cork oaks, like the one above, are numbered with the final digit of the year they were last stripped of bark.

Autumn evening near Alferce.

foresters and others with an economic interest in nature's bounty. Over towards the village of Alferce, for instance, mature deciduous trees such as chestnut and plain grow alongside pines and cork oaks. Deciduous trees used to grow much more abundantly all over the Serra de Monchique. Along with the now extinct forests that once surrounded the whole of the Mediterranean region, their destruction was brought about to make way for crops, to burn as fuel and to provide building material.

Pinewood, faster growing and thus more readily replaceable, has been in demand in the Algarve at least as far back as the 12th century and the earliest days of the Portuguese navy. It is known that the huge pine forests around Leira, north of Lisbon, were planted in the 13th and 14th centuries by Dinis I, "the farmer king," to produce wood for shipbuilding. It seems very probable that Serra de Monchique pine was extensively used by the builders of Henry the Navigator's ships at Lagos in the 15th century. By the 16th century, the demand for timber for ships had become immense. So had the demand for pitch and resin which the pine could also provide. Palaeobotanists have found evidence of pine trees and cork oaks growing wild in southern Portugal more than 4,000 years ago. With the development of more and more domestic and industrial uses for processed cork bark, the number of trees under cultivation has steadily increased over the past 300 or 400 years. Eucalyptus, on the other hand, is a relative newcomer and a highly contentious one at that. It was introduced from Australia about 100 years ago and has since assumed huge commercial importance because of the phenomenally fast growth of the trees and the voracious appetite of the paper industry. Eucalyptus poles are also widely used in the construction industries and for rural fencing. Stacked eucalyptus poles are a commonplace roadside sight anywhere in the Serra de Monchique but what is not so obvious, perhaps, is the insidious depletion of soil nutrients and subterranean water resources caused by these antipodean interlopers. Another unfortunate aspect of these commercially managed forests is that they do not promote the build-up of decomposition and intricate ecological food chains. Little secondary growth within rows upon tight rows of eucalyptus trees means few insects, which in turn means few birds or mammals.

Mountain produce

The most characteristic large shrub of the Serra de Monchique is the *arbutus* or strawberry tree which thrives on stony ground, often among heather, lavender and rosemary. The fruits of the strawberry tree are the raw material for the Algarve's most characteristic alcoholic drink, *medronho*. It is roughly akin to French kirsch and German kirschwasser. It could also be loosely likened to Scandinavia schnapps, Mexican tequila and Irish potheen. It is "a drop of the hard stuff" consumed neat, straight down the hatch, to fairly swift effect. You will see various brands of neatly labelled, commercially produced bottles of *medronho* on sale in all supermarkets and bars, but the connoisseurs do not rate any of this very highly. The real *medronho*, they insist, is the moonshine which you can only acquire privately.

The trail in search of genuine, home-made *medronho* invariably leads into the quieter reaches of the Serra de Monchique where it is made unobtrusively from January to May. Thin columns of smoke rising from dilapidated cottages

Ripening arbutus berries.

medronho dreamer.

tucked away in the folds of wooded hillsides give the game away. This is the tell-tale sign that distilling activity is in progress. The vivid red berries of the *arbutus* bushes are collected in October and November. Since care is taken to pick only perfectly ripe fruit, each bush has to be visited several times. As the bushes grow uncultivated, often on steep as well an stony ground, the beginning of the *medronho* process is hard work. Then there is a lull after the berries have been placed in wooden casks or concrete vats and left to ferment. If the fruit is sufficiently juicy, fermentation starts spontaneously. Otherwise, water is added to help things along. After a fortnight, the berries have bubbled and frothed themselves into a mushy mess. The 'must' as it is called, is then covered and kept airtight with a sheet of plastic. A careful eye and nose are kept on the must to ensure it remains moist and sweet over a period of two to four months, until it is ready to be transferred to a big copper still heated from below by a log fire.

Copper stills of various sizes are readily available at 'artisanato' shops as functional souvenirs.

The boiling point of alcohol is 78.3°C while the boiling point of water is 100 °C. Therein lies the secret of a process pioneered by the Chinese at least 3,000 years ago and more or less perfected by every tribe on earth ever since. The heated alcohol in the must vaporises and thus separates from the water. The alcohol vapour rises and is condensed in a pipe running through a tub of coolant water. At one end of the pipe you have a relatively weak alcoholic liquid. Emerging from the other end you have a strong one. Success depends largely on accurate temperature control which is achieved by *medronho* makers not with a thermometer, but by the judicious nudging of a burning log with the toe of a boot. A steady trickle of alcohol flows from the condenser pipe into an earthenware jug. The experts can fairly accurately judge the strength of the end product by shaking a small glassful and observing the bubbles that form on the surface. Large, long lasting bubbles are the hallmark of quality.

Private *medronho* makers take a week or so off

Mimosa is at its best in the Monchique mountains in late February and early March.

their normal work each year to distil enough for themselves and their friends, with perhaps some left over for illicit sale, which in the Serra de Monchique does not seem to be considered much of a sin. Apart from the bubble test, a simple way to check that you are getting good quality is to rub a little *medronho* on the back of the hand. If it smells of figs it is not pure and is most likely commercially bulk-produced. Almost all commercially or privately produced *medronho* is perfectly clear, like vodka or gin, but don't turn your nose up at yellow-tinted *medronho* should you be lucky enough to come across it. The yellow tint denotes a beverage of rare quality which has rested for a year at least in an oak cask.

Ground floor bargains.

Those who regularly imbibe good *medronho* claim that it is a "happy" drink free from the effects of depression ascribed to gin, or the aggression sometimes brought on by whisky. Furthermore, they say, there is no "morning after" hangover provided you drink only *medronho* and no other form of alcohol. Copious amounts of *medronho* on top of either wine or beer in the same evening is another story, however. Forestry workers and farmers have *medronho* and black coffee for breakfast. *Medronho*, honey and hot water is said to be good for staving off colds. To make a delicious cocktail, you can mix medronho with liquidised melon and crushed ice. Finally, for the real masochists, there is another *medronho* cocktail appropriately called

Presunto and chouriço

Winter waters.

arrasa miudas, which translates into "brain dissolver." It is very easy to make: equal portions of *medronho* and Port wine. It is very tasty and very potent. Two of these are at least one too many.

As you travel through the Serra de Monchique, from time to time you will get a whiff of pigs. They are raised in fair numbers, more so here than anywhere else in the Algarve. The Portuguese have always been partial to pork meat in all its forms. As refrigeration is a comparitively recent innovation inland and does not yet extend to all parts of the *serra* region, it is natural that cured ham, *presunto*, is a speciality. The time-honoured way of curing a leg of pork is to completely bed it in salt for several months. You will find whole *presuntos* hanging in some of the *tabernas*. Ask for a small portion. A few slices with a chunk of fresh, home-made bread makes a good starter to a chicken lunch, or an appetising snack with a cool drink. Something else which tastes good with a chunk of bread is *chouriço*, a strongly flavoured type of cured pork sausage. It is especially tasty in soups and stews or grilled in alcohol flame. Generally speaking, pork is of good quality in the Algarve whatever way it is prepared or served.

Urban householders, citrus growers and vegetable farmers in the foothills and coastal plain all have good reason to be grateful for the Serra de Espinhaço de Cão and the Serra de Monchique. Not only do the hills mellow the climate by acting as a shield against cold northerly winds, but they provide the catchment area for much needed water in a low rainfall zone. Streams, nearly all of them seasonal, feed into the Bravura and Arade reservoirs in winter and early spring, providing enough water for the rest of the year.

A recommended scenic route out of the Serra de Monchique starts at the village of Alferce and the road signposted Fornalha and Monchicão. It runs alongside a deep, thickly vegetated gorge at the bottom of which gurgles one of the Algarve's permanent streams. This is the headwater of the Odelouca river which eventually empties into the estuary at Portimão.

The road - unsurfaced but usually alright - follows the river as far as the N124 between Portimão and Silves.

Silves, Crusaders and Moors

*I*t was from the Portimão direction that the Crusaders approached Silves in the 12th century but instead of by road, the Crusaders came by river. In the Middle Ages the river at Silves was much more than the trickle it is today. It was navigable almost up to the fortress which then loomed over the town just as it does now. From the direction of Portimão, however, the castle looks at its least impressive. Viewed from the east as you arrive from São Bartolomeu de Messines, or from the south coming from Lagoa, you are faced with an imposing red sandstone edifice which would look neat on a chocolate box, but daunting to a would-be invader. Pretty and placid as it looks now, Silves castle was the venue for appalling carnage as Christians and Muslims lay siege to each other and fought horrific hand-to-hand battles.

While Muslim Portugal as a whole was ruled from Seville, the regional capital of al-Garb was Silves, then known as Xelb, Shalb or Chelb. According to

Silves time warp.

Page Opposite: long gone are the golden minarets. This is the skyline of Silves today.

the Muslim geographer, Idrisi, Silves in the mid-12th century was "fine in appearance with attractive buildings and well furnished bazaars." It was a port with a shipyard and a thriving trade with African and Mediterranean ports, dealing mainly in fruit and fish. The people of Silves spoke pure Arabic. They were said to be particularly eloquent and fond of writing poetry. Both the upper and lower classes, said Idrisi, were elegantly mannered. It is, perhaps, significant that Idrisi had far less to say about Lisbon which he dismissed as "a compact and well-defended town."

Well-defended Lisbon certainly was in 1140 when its Muslim inhabitants resisted an attack by the Portuguese forces of King Afonso Henriques assisted by 70 shiploads of English and Norman Crusaders bound for Palestine. Seven years later, a fleet of 164 vessels with about 13,000 English, German and Flemish Crusaders arrived en route to the Holy Land from Dartmouth. After much haggling, a contract was signed between the Crusaders and Afonso Henriques in which the king agreed to hand over all the spoils looted from Lisbon in return for the Crusaders' help. Land was also offered to any Crusaders who might want to settle in Portugal afterwards. Spurred on by these inducements, the combined armies managed to capture Lisbon after a siege lasting 17 weeks. Gilbert, a Crusader from Hastings, was installed as the first bishop of the restored see. As it turned out, the capture of Lisbon was not only a major milestone in the Christian reconquest of Portugal, it was the only real success during the second Crusade which ended with a frustrating and fruitless siege of Damascus. It was also a prelude to momentous events at Silves.

Defending the faith.

Although they shared the same religion, the Moors were far from being a homogeneous people. They were a mixture of Arabs and Berbers from various parts of North Africa. In the first half of the 12th century, for example, the land between Beja and Faro was said to be inhabited by Egyptians, while from Faro to Seville was Syrian territory. At the same time, the well-established empire of the Almoravid Muslims was in decline and under growing threat from the reformist

Almohads who advocated a Berberised form of Islam. There was a great deal of racial and tribal friction. By about the middle of the 12th century, the Almohads had gained supremacy in Seville and Granada, Beja and Évora. Ibn Qasi, a native of Silves, governor of the Algarve and a self-proclaimed Mahdi, sought the Portuguese king's help against the Almohad expansion, but his own people rose against him. They killed him and impaled his head on the point of a lance which was publicly paraded in Silves to chants of: "Behold, the

Close by the castle today.

Mahdi of the Christians.''

Lances about two metres in length and tapering to a slender point were the main weapons carried by Muslim horsemen. They also carried straight swords. Muslim infantrymen of the period carried straight swords or curved scimitars made from the finest Damascus or Toledo steel. Javelins, bows and daggers were among the other weapons used by the soldiers of Allah who, by fighting the Christians, were seeking their own salvation. Likewise, the Crusaders with their battle axes, pikes and spiked maces, sought eternal reward for their defence of Christendom against the Islamic infidels. Led by knights of noble breeding, the Crusaders were also very keen on earthly rewards. Their deeds of great devotion and daring were often followed by ruthless raping and pillaging.

There were eight Crusades in all to the Holy Land, three of which - the second, third and fifth - had a major bearing on Portugal. Portugal's position on the sea route to Palestine meant it was inevitable that Crusaders from north-west Europe would call in for provisions and thus become embroiled in the national affairs of a Christian country occupied by Muslims. Such a stop-over during the third Crusade in 1189 made the reconquest of Silves possible. The Crusaders' fleet put into Lisbon harbour in July. A deal was struck with King Sancho I. A combined Portuguese, English, German and Flemish fleet sailed on to the Algarve. On the fourth day out of Lisbon they sailed up the Arade river and anchored close to Silves which could be seen to be a prosperous if not opulent Muslim city of 20,000 or 30,000 inhabitants. Those living in the lower part of the town quickly fled to the better protected upper part. As the Christians pressed their attack, burning everything in their path, the Muslims took sanctuary within the castle walls.

Apart from its historical significance, Silves is best know for the citrus orchards around it. Portugal's finest oranges and lemons are grown in the fertile valleys east of the town and in the neighbourhood of villages like Malhão and Algoz.

Once the drawbridge went up on a fortress like that in Silves, there were three basic ways of forcing those inside to surrender. The attackers had to get into the fortress by either going under or over the walls. Going under meant mining and tunnelling. Going over called for long, scaling ladders or the construction of

Page opposite:
peace within the castle walls.

movable towers with flaps which could be lowered on to the top of the ramparts. The third option was to starve the enemy into capitulation while harassing them by lobbing rocks and the medieval equivalent of Molotov cocktails over the walls with crude catapult machines. All of this went on during the 1189 siege of Silves with varying degrees of success. At one stage the Christians mined their way into underground galleries beneath the castle, but the Moors managed to repulse them after brutal hand-to-hand fighting. The fate of the defenders was sealed when the Christians managed to mine their way in again and cut off the main water supply. It was then only a matter of time before the Muslims gave in. Six weeks after the start of the siege, the Muslims offered to surrender if they were allowed to leave with whatever possessions they could carry. Sancho I agreed, but the Crusaders welshed on the deal. The They allowed the Muslims to leave, but first stripped them of their belongings. As the Muslims trekked off towards Seville, the Crusaders went on a looting rampage. After the third day of this, Sancho I was so appalled that he ordered the Crusaders out of the castle and back to their ships.

Economic benefits were offered as inducements in the recruitment of Crusaders. Many thousands joined the third Crusade chiefly to avoid paying their taxes or interest on their taxes at home. So these were mercenary minded men right from the start. Without them, though, Portugal had great problems in coping with the Almohads. The summer after the first siege of Silves, the Almohad caliph of Seville dispatched a fleet to retake the city. That this attack failed was partly due to the fortuitous arrival in Lisbon of a Palestine-bound fleet under the command of England's Richard I. Coeur de Lion, the Lionheart, as he was nicknamed, sent a contingent of men-at-arms to help with the defence of Silves. The following summer, however, Richard's forces were in Acre in the Kingdom of Jerusalem when the Moors returned once more to Silves to exact revenge for their 1189 humiliation. Silves fell to the Muslims in a month and all of

Sitio de Fontes, a popular picnicking spot between Silves and Estombar.

Sancho I's previous victories south of the River Tagus were nullified as the Almohads swept through southern Portugal leaving towns in ruins. Almost another six decades were to pass before Silves, Faro and the rest of the towns in the Algarve were finally retaken and secured by the Christians under Afonso III.

The bloody sieges of the 12th and 13th centuries form only a part of Silves castle's colourful history which has its origins in pre-Roman times. Information about the successive phases of its existence is being uncovered in an on-going programme of archaeological excavations. Restored to its present form in 1835, the castle with its peaceful gardens of jacarandas and oleanders nowadays reveals no hint of either the sumptuousness or the savagery that once existed within its mighty walls, except for a statue of Afonso III. The only reminders of the Muslims are a 65-metre-deep Moorish well and the vaulted roof of the huge cistern isolated during the siege of 1189 and still in use by the town council today. The nearest the castle gets to becoming even slightly rowdy these days is during the annual summer beer festival held here.

Close by the castle is Silves Cathedral, mostly whitewashed but pointed in the dark red sandstone of the region. The cathedral, modest in size, replaced a mosque at the time of the reconquest, but much of its original Gothic was replaced during successive rebuildings. Its importance diminished, as did the

Above: Silves' Ponte Romana.
Right: Silves cathedral.

whole city's, when the bishopric was moved from Silves to Faro in the 16th century. The cathedral still has some tombs of Crusaders and a memorial stone to King João II who was buried here after his death in Alvor. His remains were later removed to the magnificent abbey at Batalha in central Portugal. Entrance to the cathedral is by a side door rather than by the main arched doorway . Nearby is a neat little museum.

The other ecclesiastical monument of interest in Silves is on the main roadside on the way out of town towards São Bartolomeu de Messines. It is the so-called Cross of Portugal about which there is much

A signposted turn-off on the road from Silves to São Bartolomeu de Messines leads to the Barragem do Arade, one of the region's four major reservoirs, set among the cistus and eucalyptus-covered foothills of the Serra de Monchique. The reservoir water is used for irrigating crops, especially oranges.
Photo: Margaret Daughtrey.

185

speculation but little hard fact. It is a carved limestone cross thought to have been made in the 16th century. One side depicts the Crucifixion, the other Christ's descent from the cross.

São Bartolomeo de Messines

*T*hough not as grand as when gleaming minarets pierced its skyline 800 years ago, Silves today is quite a busy place. In particular it is a centre of citrus cultivation and cork processing. It is only a small provincial town but it is decidedly up-tempo compared with the next town along to the east. São Bartolomeu de Messines, rather a mouthful even if Portuguese is your mother tongue, is usually abbreviated to Messines. It is as relaxed and pleasant a country town as you will find anywhere in southern Portugal. The town's high street passes an old and unusual parish church surrounded by 17th and 18th century houses of simple, striking design. The squat, robust church, nicely restored, was in existence during the last quarter of the 16th century, though it may be even older. The date above the front doorway, 1716, refers to one of several major renovation jobs. Others were in 1778 and 1787. The twisted columns

Messines church.

separating the aisles and on either side of the front doorway are characteristic of the earliest Manueline period. Not far from the church is the birthplace of Messines' most famous son, the nationally acclaimed poet João de Deus (1830 - 1896). He was a quiet, reserved man and his best known collection of poems, *A Field of Flowers,* reflects the simplicity and charm still to be found in Messines and the surrounding countryside.

Alte, 11 km east of Messines, has its own celebrated poet, Candido Guerreiro (1871 - 1953). Some of his verse is displayed on painted tile panels at a popular picnicking spot by a leafy stream at the bottom of the village. Much older tiles, some of them made in Seville in the 16th century, adorn the chapels inside the nearby parish church which has a fine Manueline portal. Widely known in Portugal for the standard of its folk music and dance groups, Alte is still proud of the national recognition it was given in 1938 when the ministry of information placed it second in a country-wide most attractive "typical" village competition. Another thing Alte is proud about is the

A field of flowers.

quality of its spring water. It is said to account for the health and longevity of the locals. Only fit and healthy visitors armed with a bottle of water should bother asking directions to the Buraco dos Mouros, a place of interest about an hour's trek from the village. It is a huge, three-chambered cave, once a hiding place for Moors, now a breeding place for bats.

Moorish influences

*T*here was a good deal of warring between the Christians and the Moors in the Middle Ages, as we have already noted, but there was a good deal of peaceful co-existence too. In northern Portugal the forces of militant Christianity regained control quite quickly after the initial Moorish invasion in the 8th century, but nearly 500 years passed before anything similar happened in the far south. While the ideal of ultimate reconquest of their own country was always present, the Portuguese in the south of the country became closely entwined culturally and economically with their occupiers. A lot rubs off in the course of 500 years and some of it can still be seen in the countryside around Alte and many other places inland.

Being a desert people, the Moors were keenly aware of the need to make efficient use of limited supplies of what is arguably the single most valuable natural resource anywhere: water. They introduced a system of irrigation in which water was distributed to the furrows between growing crops via canals and aqueducts fed from deep wells. The Arabs were masters at building wells and it was the Arabs who first devised a mechanical method of drawing from them. It consisted of a large, vertical wheel positioned above the well, driven through a simple cog arrangement by oxen yolked to a horizontal shaft. Two parallel loops of rope with buckets suspended between them at close intervals passed over the wheel and down into the well. As the wheel turned, the buckets went down empty, submerged and came up on the other side full. At the top of the wheel the buckets tipped and their contents flowed either into holding tanks or straight to the fields. Arab wells are still in use in rural areas of the Algarve today and very similar devices for drawing water,

A Moorish invention made redundant not that long ago by pumps and plastic pipes.

though made of iron and turned by donkeys, were in constant use until a few years ago. A few have been adapted to diesel power. Most stand idle and rusting.

The Moors were also keenly aware of the destructive power of water on agricultural land. Top soil was liable to be loosened and swept away when steep slopes were battered by the heavy rains of winter. To combat this

Page opposite:
terrace farming.

sort of erosion, as well as to make slopes much more manageable for growing crops, the Moors constructed terraces - level plots of land in stepped tiers which could be irrigated in a controlled way. Such terraces are still in widespread use to grow a wide variety of crops some of which, such as oranges and lemons, were introduced to Portugal by the Moors.

Another common inland sight with a probable Moorish connection are abandoned windmills. Although windmills seem to have been first used in the Middle East in the 7th century or earlier, they did not make an appearance in Western Europe until near the close of the 12th century. Some historians credit the Crusaders with bringing the earliest windmills plans back to Europe, but it seems more likely that in southern Portugal and Spain they were introduced directly by the Arabs. The typical Algarvean windmill consisted of a fixed round-house tower with triangular sails wrapped around poles braced to a bowsprit which stuck out in front of a movable, conical top or "cap." The sails were faced squarely into the wind. Through a cog system, not unlike that of the well wheels, the sails drove a pair of millstones between which the grain was ground. A few windmills on exposed hilltops have been restored, some incorporated into houses, but all that remains of most are abandoned stone towers.

Last turn.

Loulé

Inside Loulé market.

Not much is left of the Moorish castle captured in 1248 which stands on a lonely hillside near the village of Paderne, but there is a strong, lingering aura of the Middle Ages hanging over the castle ruins and the stream winding through the valley below. To those susceptible to such sensations, Paderne and other quieter reaches of the Algarve seem steeped in benign spirits of past ages. These spirits, however, have difficulty surviving amid the bustle of the region's largest inland town, Loulé, present population about 15,000. Loulé castle is Moorish in origin, perhaps older, but unlike Paderne it is far from being deserted. The little that is left of it has been surrounded by relatively modern buildings near the town centre. Its crenellated walls, barrel-vaulted ceilings and some of the monograms of

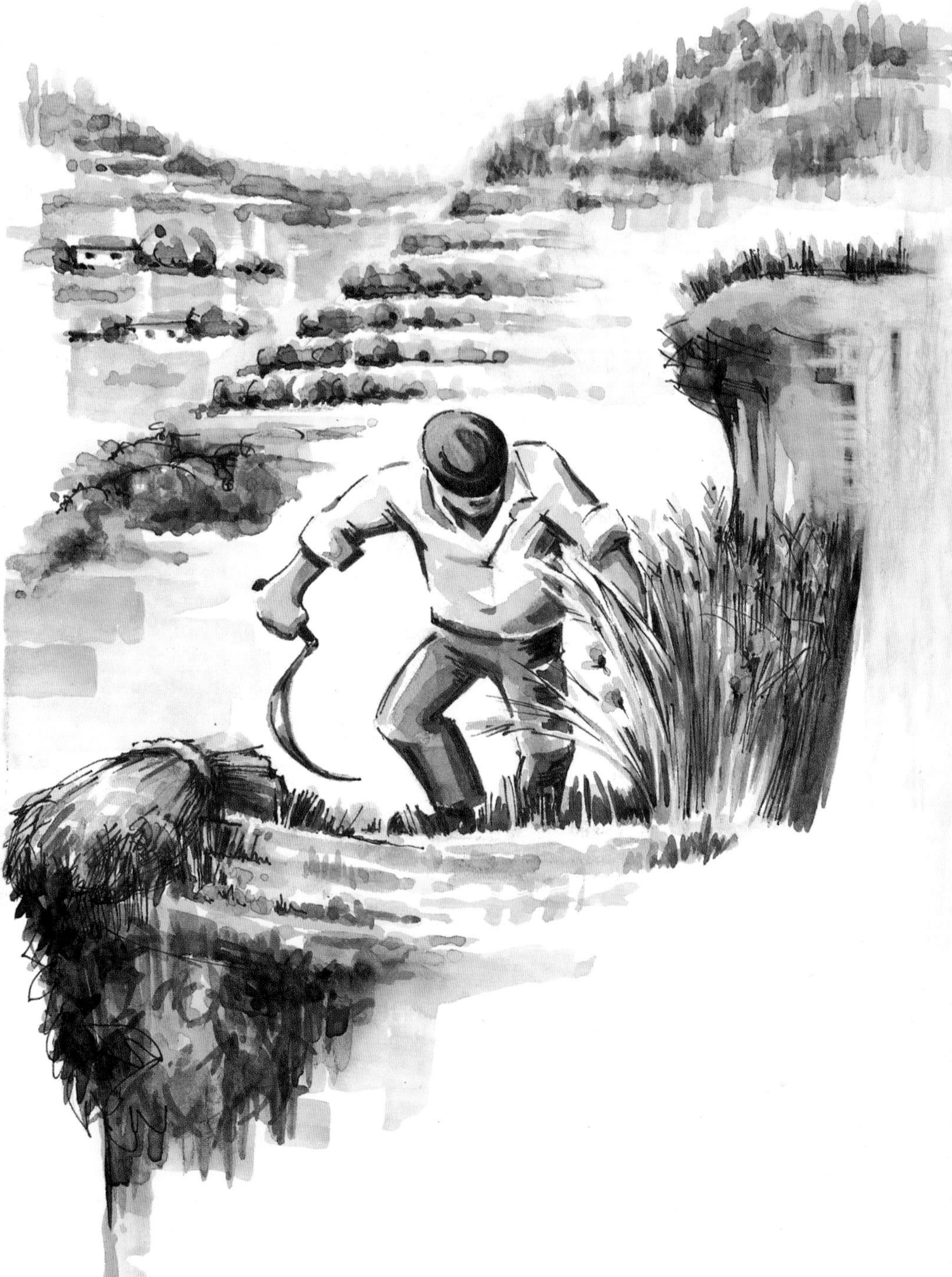

From the outside, Loulé market looks a bit Moorish.

Days of glory are gone...

the medieval masons who worked on them have been restored and preserved. The castle remnants are now a carefully kept museum. It is a good starting point for a short walk through the old part of town.

You can probably pick up a map of the town from the tourist information office in the forecourt of the castle and the *alcaidaria* , the fortress governor's quarters. The street immediately outside is named after D. Paio Peres Correia, master of the Knights of Santiago, who captured this and other important castles in southern Portugal from the Moors. Bearing right you come into Largo D. Pedro I (a *largo*, incidentally, is a small square, a *praça* is a big one). You can either continue on around to Largo Afonso III at the back of the castle, or head in the opposite direction towards the nearby Church of São Clemente. Either way, as you mosey along the narrow streets you will come across small, dimly lit workshops making and selling brass and copperware, leather goods, wrought iron, wooden and cane furniture, esparto hats and handbags. Loulé has been a town of artisans since the capture of the castle - and probably for much longer.

The church is a mixture of styles dating from 13th-century Gothic . It has some late Manueline flourishes. Together with the peaceful little square around it and the tiny park opposite the main Gothic portal, this is a

corner of quiet charm. The same could hardly be said of the nearby municipal market, an outlandish building of arabesque design. It is the town's main centre of hubbub each weekday morning, reaching a crescendo on Saturday mornings when the whole operation overflows into the surrounding streets and all manner of goods are on offer at very cheap prices. More stylish and fashionable goods are sold in the smart shops and boutiques along the main thoroughfare, Praça da República leading to the Avenida José da Costa Mealha, which is lined with lime and Judas trees providing bright colour in spring and shade in summer.

Early springtime in Loulé is when the locals let their hair down, which they are wont to do more than any other townsfolk in the Algarve. Carnival, five days of merrymaking before the 40 days and nights of Lent, is widely but rather feebly celebrated in the Algarve - except in Loulé. It is not quite up to Rio de Janeiro standard, but the people of Loulé put a bit of effort into their Carnival festivities which attract participants and spectators from the whole district and beyond. Foreign visitors should be warned that there is slightly more to the merrymaking than parades with colourful floats, fancy dress, dancing in the streets and heavier than normal drinking. Youths delight in showering onlookers, especially girls, with flour and paint and committing other dastardly pranks.

Nothing like this happens at the colourful but much more solemn, annual Mãe Soberana celebrations. It is one of the region's foremost *romarias* or religious processions. A 16th-century image of Mãe Soberana (the Sovereign Mother) is carried into the town on Easter Sunday from a shrine on a hill about a kilometre to the west. The return procession a week later is enjoyed even more by the crowds lining the route, but rather less by the bearers who have to carry the heavy image back up the steep slope leading to the shrine. Then in June, Loulé celebrates its patron saint's day. Every town and village has a patron saint's day. In Loulé, as in almost every other town, it is marked by exploding rockets before breakfast and a fireworks display at night, with plenty of public fun in between.

Copperwork.

193

Estói

*T*hirteen kilometres to the east, São Brás de Alportel is an altogether more subdued little town in the heart of some of the Algarve's most enchanting countryside. It is halfway between the hills and the sea. Farther south, in the village of Estói, visitors may find the prevailing mood melancholic. Estói is best known for its nearby Roman ruins and its derelict *palácio* .

The palace at Estói is all the more intriguing because, at the time of writing, you can get no closer to it than the outer rambling gardens. A side entrance near the parish church (the front wrought-iron gates are kept locked) leads along a palm-shaded avenue past stables and byres to the front terrace of the *palácio.* Here a rococo bandstand overlooks an ornamental pool the centre-piece of which is a group of voluptuous marble maidens. The saucy theme is continued in surrounding blue and white *azulejos* and bas-relief sculptures. Among the busts of prominent people, that of the poet Milton is given pride of place. Figurines, all but hidden in an alcove behind coloured glass doors, make up an elaborate nativity scene. Twin flights of ballustraded steps lead down to a grotto with statues of Venus, Diana and the Three Graces. Similar steps lead up to a forecourt which is flanked by coloured glass gazebos and heavily creepered walls surmounted by more busts, including those of Goethe, Moltke and Bismarck. Yet more sculptured figures sit atop the anaemic pink facade. The place has been crying out for renovation for years. For years there has been talk of it, but at the time of writing nothing has been done.

A shaded avenue past stables and byres.

Among the most precious as well as the most easily overlooked adornments in the grounds of the *palácio* are mosaics which were presumably robbed from the nearby *ruinas Romanas* . Over the years, the ruins have been extensively plundered for private collections, but now they are fenced off with set hours for public viewing which don't seem to be strictly adhered to. Archaeologists, including teams from Germany, have carried out much work on the site. They have established that a succession of buildings were constructed here from the 1st century AD. One large section of the ruins shows the characteristic form of a Roman peristyle villa with a gallery of columns around a courtyard or garden. Large rooms were luxuriously paved with mosaics in a wide range of geometric motifs. On the west side of the peristyle, next to a large dining-room, was a bathing suite comprising a changing-room with benches for anointing and massaging, and hot and cold bathrooms. The tepidarium and caldarium had floor heating by means of hot air passed through underground chambers from cauldrons of boiling water in a furnace room on the north side of the bathing suite. The frigidarium had a circular marble basin for cooling off after the hot tub. Archaeologists can see all of this clearly. Alas, to the untrained eye it may seem no more than a maze of foundation walls and some faded mosaic decoration.

The Romans often decorated their baths with fish mosaics.

There was a street on the south side of the villa which separated it from an imposing building, the surviving wall of which, just right of the entrance to the site, is Milreu's most outstanding feature. This was a Roman nymphaerium, a specialised temple devoted to the cult of water. Archaeological excavations have revealed that the Visigoths turned it into a church complete with a Christian baptismal font and a small mausoleum. The close proximity of the water sanctuary was unusual for a Roman villa and so too were some of the decorative ornaments found in the house: well-preserved busts in marble of Empress Agrippina (1st century AD), Emperor Hadrian (2nd century) and Emperor Gallien (3rd century). They are now in the Faro and Lagos Museums.

In the first few centuries after Christ, the villa at Milreu was obviously no ordinary house. It was the home of noblemen. Relative to the times, it was at least on a par with the millionaires' residences in the most exclusive developments on the south coast today. It was infinitely better in real terms than most of the ordinary homes now occupied in the neighbourhood nearly 2,000 years on.

Country cottages

The basic rural cottage in the Algarve consists of four rooms, each three or four metres square, with a front door and two small windows. There are two bedrooms, a sitting-room and a kitchen, but no bathroom or toilet. The walls are made of stones bound with mud. They are rendered and whitewashed inside and out. Pitched roofs are tiled and underlayed with a row of cane. There is likely to be a fireplace and it will be in the kitchen and used for cooking, not heating. Portuguese country folk do not heat their homes in winter because they believe that sudden changes of temperature when moving between the warm of inside and cold of outside cause illness. Many cottages still rely on water delivered by truck, stored rainwater or wells; many connected to the mains have only a single tap outside which is not plumbed into the house. Electrification is now widespread, but for some people the paraffin lamp is still a standard domestic appliance.

Immediately in front of Algarve cottages there is usually a stone bench. Of all of the fittings and fixtures, this is one of the most important. In the mild months it is a place to sit down with family and friends to chat or just ponder the world. However simple their life-style, the country folk know a thing or two about the world at large because the few pieces of furniture inside their home almost invariably include a TV set. Apart from a mandatory crucifix and a few family pictures inside, the most important domestic adornment is outside on the roof. The Algarve is famous for its chimney designs even though they are not always practical. The more intricate chimney patterns are extremely pretty, but it is doubtful if they let the smoke out. As for sanitation and matters of personal hygiene, such things don't overly bother country folk either. The Romans of Milreu would probably find their 20th-century neighbours somewhat primitive in some respects.

Most ordinary village houses are not all that much better off than the country cottages. True, they have water, electricity and even a rudimentary bathroom, but they are very cramped, especially for families living with in-laws or grandparents, which is not unusual in

a relatively poor society which places high importance on the family unit and the care of the elderly. One thing in their favour is that the fixed rents on older properties are very low. What a contrast all this is to the foreign-owned villas that have mushroomed along the south coast and, in more recent years, in certain inland areas as well. Britons and to a lesser extent other nationalities have been buying land and building houses in which to settle, or as second homes for holidays and perhaps eventual retirement. These *estrangeiros* have come to expect at least as many bathrooms as bedrooms, fitted kitchens with high-tech appliances, solar energy to heat the water, satellite dishes to receive TV programmes in their own language, automatic irrigation in landscaped gardens and, of course, private swimming pools. No doubt the noblemen of Milreu would have approved.

North-east Algarve

*T*he roads running north from Loulé past the stalactite caves of Querença, and from São Brás de Alportel past a hillside pousada of the same name, meet at Barranco do Velho. Not much else happens at Barranco do Velho though there are fine views from the curiously abandoned Miradoura de Caldeirão, a good place for a picnic. Anyone who talks glibly about the Algarve being "a building site" or "totally spoilt" has never been to Barranco do Velho, let alone up the road that winds its peaceful way through the eastern

São Brás de Alportel from the pousada on a hill just outside of town.

Caldeirão hills towards the nearly comatosed village of Cachopo. Here you are getting into the heart of that huge tract of sparsely populated farmland and wilderness that makes up the north-eastern sector of the Algarve. It is an area of about 1,500 square kilometres, well over a quarter of the entire province, bounded in the south by São Brás de Alportel and Castro Marim, and in the north by Ameixial and Alcoutim.

About 5 km after Barranco do Velho you pass an oleander filled ravine cut by the upper reaches of the Odeleite river which eventually finds its way to the Guadiana. A few kilometres on, just past the hamlet of Montes Novos, the road emerges on top of the *serra* on a plateau which in April and May is covered in blooming *cistus* rock roses and splashed with brilliant yellow broom. If you turn off this road, at the Castelão signpost for example, you are turning into another age. Castelão, like many of the remote hamlets up here, is a tight, unplanned cluster of low, stone houses and similar adjoining outhouses for the goats and chickens. It is a scene straight out of biblical times. They grow wheat around the village, but the slopes are too steep for tractors and the farmers are too poor to afford them, so the sowing and reaping and baling is done torturously by hand just as it has been since time immemorial. It is

Natural blending....
Top: cottage of stone and thatch near Cachopo.

Above right: chameleons.
Photos: Parque Natural da Ria Formosa.

199

Page opposite:
the view from Alcoutim.
Below left: last stop.
Bottom: frontier friends.

reminiscent of the Rif Mountains in Morocco. It certainly has little in common with Faro or Quarteira or exclusive developments like Quinta do Lago little more than 40 km away.

For those who really want to get away from it all and close to nature, take to the untarred roads - but take care. Make sure you have enough petrol to get back to civilisation. Roadside springs can be found here and there to sake the thirst during the searing hot days of high summer, but secondary roads may become impassable to all but four-wheel drive vehicles because of torrents in winter. Such a road is the one from just north of Cachopo to Ameixial. It supplies the hypotenuse to a marvellous triangular drive of about 65 km starting from Barranco do Velho. Otherwise, stick to the main road which sweeps up past Martim Longo and over the top of the north-eastern Algarve to deliver the more intrepid of travellers to Alcoutim, a cul-de-sac town on the banks of the Guadiana 40 km north of where the river enters the sea at Vila Real de Santo António. At both Alcoutim and the adjacent Spanish village of San Lucar de Guadiana there are castle ruins hauntingly recalling centuries of fearful vigilance across the border. The fear and loathing has gone. So have the customs men. All that separates the two communities now is a narrow stretch of placid, slow-moving water.

At your service:

Advertising section
for services and products
which can be recommended
with confidence.

Page opposite: Eventide
on a sun-blessed shore.
Photo: Nancy Denty.

CASINOS DO ALGARVE

CASINO DA ROCHA
RESERVAS (082) 23 145

CASINO DE VILAMOURA
RESERVAS (089) 30 29 99

CASINO DE MONTE GORDO
RESERVAS (081) 51 22 24

APOSTE NO DOURADO

Está com sorte.
Todo o encanto e brilho do Algarve
continuam pela noite dentro,
nos salões dos Casinos do Algarve.
A alegria e as cores dos espectáculos,
o sabor marcante da boa mesa
e as emoções do jogo esperam por si.
Venha aos Casinos. Aposte… no dourado.

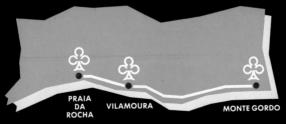

PRAIA DA ROCHA   VILAMOURA   MONTE GORDO

SOINTAL   CASINOS DO ALGARVE
RUA FILIPE FOLQUE, 2 - 6.º Esq.
1000 LISBOA Tel. (01) 352 86 00
Fax (01) 52 05 43 • Telex 16454

Ayer

Accommodation

All holiday accommodation in the Algarve is supposed to be registered with the regional tourist board. Apart from individual, independent villas and apartments, all registered accommodation is officially classified.

Types of accommodation are as follows:
HOTELS - rated 1 to 5 stars depending on the quality of the premises and facilities.
MOTELS - rated 2 or 3 stars.
ESTALAGENS - privately-run inns, rated 4 or 5 stars.
POUSADAS - state-run hotels either in historic buildings or in outstanding locations. There are only two in the Algarve.
ALBERGARIAS - 4-star guest-houses.
TURISMO RURAIS - rustic houses in suburban settings.
TURISMO DE HABITAÇÕES - Mansions or houses of special architectural interest.
PENSÕES - pensions or boarding-houses, rated between 1 and 4 stars.
RESIDENCIALS - much the same as pensões.
APARTHOTELS and *HOTEL APARTAMENTOS* combine some of the facilities of hotels with the self-catering independence of apartments.
APARTAMENTOS TURISTICOS - blocks of holiday apartments rated first, second or third class.
ALDEAMENTOS TURISTICOS - holiday developments consisting of detached villas, townhouses, apartments, or a mixture of these. They are classified deluxe, first or second class.

Prices of accommodation are publicly displayed at reception desks and in rooms. Prices depend not only on the type and quality of the accommodation, but on the time of year. The same room or villa is generally far cheaper in winter than high summer. There is no hard and fast rule on the start and finish of seasons, but the breakdown for pricing purposes is often like this:
LOW   beginning of November to end of March.
MID   April, May, June, October.
HIGH   first two weeks in July, September.
PEAK   second two weeks in July, August.

Availability depends on the season. Accommodation of all kinds is plentiful in winter and usually fairly plentiful in the mid seasons, but advance reservations are preferable, perhaps essential, in the high and peak seasons. The exception to this rule is accommodation associated with golf courses. November to April is the main golf season.

Airport

The Algarve's only international airport is a few kilometres from the provincial capital, Faro. It was opened in 1965 and since then has been extensively expanded and modernised. The present terminal was opened in 1989 and is designed to handle three million passengers a year. There are further expansion plans to cope with five million passengers annually. The airport is served by a few scheduled carriers and by many charter airlines.
On arrival:
* There are no formalities for passengers on domestic flights.
* International passengers from EC countries need to show only

their passport at immigration control.
* Customs arrangements are the same as elsewhere in Europe.   Phone numbers:

Switchboard	(089) 818281
Flight information	(089) 818982
Lost property	(089) 818302
British Airways	(089) 818181
Lufthansa	(089) 818269
TAP - Air Portugal	(089) 818539

Airstrips

There are three aerodromes suitable for light aircraft :

LAGOS	(082) 762906
MONTES ALVOR	(082) 495942
VILAMOURA	(089) 312959

Two organisations offer light plane trips and specialist charter services :

Aero Clube de Faro	(089) 823846
Aero Algarve - Penina	(082) 495828

Microlight hire and trips can be arranged by the Algarve Microlight Centre, Lagos aerodrome, open Monday to Saturday between 9.0am and midday, tel. (082) 762906.

Archaeology

There are a few museum collections and a number of sites open to the public which are of particular interest to anyone keen on archaeology. On-going annual digs are conducted at some of the sites by university groups. Here are some of the most interesting places to visit:

CASTRO MARIM - Greek, Roman and Moorish relics have been found within the largest of Castro Marim's two hilltop fortresses.   Much rebuilt and renovated outer ramparts encompass a 12th-century castle, the first headquarters of the Order of Christ, the religious - military order which succeeded the Knights Templar.

FARO - Housed in a 16th-century convent building, the Archaeological Museum in Faro has the Algarve's largest collection of ancient artefacts, including much material from Faro itself, formerly the Roman town of Ossonoba.

MILREU - The extensive Roman ruins here are of a peristyle villa and water sanctuary built and rebuilt a number of times during the first three centuries A.D.

VILAMOURA - Excavations at the Cerro da Vila site near the marina have yielded Roman, Visigothic and Moorish relics which may be viewed in a small, on-site museum.

SILVES - The Moorish capital of the Algarve is still dominated by a magnificent, red sandstone castle which is still being studied. The central feature of Silves Museum is an *in situ* Moorish well.

ALCALAR - The earliest evidence of civilisation in the region is to be found in a fenced area of countryside about 5 km north of the Penina Hotel in the form of neolithic dolmens.

LAGOS - The first gallery of the Regional Museum next to the ornate Church of São António is devoted to relics dating from very early civilisation through the Roman, Visigothic and Moorish periods. The old town walls, constructed and enlarged over the centuries, date back to the beginning of the millennium.

MARTINHAL - Excavations a few years ago revealed Roman pottery kilns on a scale suggesting a settlement of considerable size on the edge of Promontorium Sacrum. Natural erosion is fast destroying what is left of the kilns on the edge of low cliffs.

The **Algarve Archaeological Association** (Associação Arqueológica do Algarve), with more than 170 mostly English-speaking members, encourages the wider appreciation of history and archaeology in Portugal and especially the Algarve. It arranges occasional field trips and holds monthly meetings (except in July and August) which interested visitors are welcome to attend.

Astronomy

The Algarve's 37° latitude means that more of the night sky can be seen from here than from locations in Britain or other northern European countries. Much less cloud, less artificial light, shorter twilight with longer summer nights are other advantages for visiting astronomers.

The sole organisation specialising in services to visiting amateur astronomers and their families is the Centre for Observational Astronomy in the Algarve (COAA). It is an informal field study centre run by an English couple, Dr Bev and Janet Ewen-Smith. Brochures can be obtained from the centre at Casa Adelina, Poio, Mexilhoeira Grande, 8500 Portimão. Tel. (082) 471180.

Banks
See also: Currency

Normal banking hours are Monday to Friday 8.30am to 3.00pm. Exchange banks at Faro airport and the frontier at Villa Real do Santo António remain open at weekends and public holidays. Their opening and closing times correspond with the first and last aircraft and ferries.

Banks in all tourist areas prominently display the current exchange rates for most European and other major currencies. The rate for travellers' cheques is slightly higher than for notes. Cash advances can usually be obtained with Mastercard, Eurocard, Access, Visa and other credit cards.

Beaches
See companion map (sold separately) *Insiders Tourist Map of the Algarve.*

Nowhere in the Algarve is far from a beach and there are more than 60 named beaches to choose from. Albufeira, for example, has eight within a short drive. There are another eight in the vicinity of Carvoeiro. Sagres has four. Monte Gordo has only one but it continues under different names for almost 20 km. All of the Algarve's sandy *praias* are of a golden colour not found in the Mediterranean, They are swept clean by the tides of the cooler but far less polluted Atlantic.

Many of the beaches are individually mentioned in the book under the headings of the towns or villages they are nearest to, but here are a few general pointers:

In the eastern half of the province, between Vila Real de Santo António and Quarteira, the beaches are all long, open strands. They are mostly on low-lying islands. Between Quarteira and Sagres, long beaches with dunes are outnumbered by bays and coves backed by fantastically eroded cliffs. Up the west coast, from Sagres northwards, the cliffs are darker coloured and more formidable. The spectacular beaches here lie exposed to Atlantic rollers and surf.

The most crowded beaches are those

closest to the towns and popular resorts on the south coast. On long beaches the crowds usually thin out considerably the farther you walk along the sand away from the main point of access. The least crowded beaches are on the west coast, and those on the south coast which are difficult to get to.

Topless bathing is commonplace; on some of the most popular beaches it is the norm. Nudism is not unusual; it is legally accepted on secluded beaches.

You can virtually step out of your car on to most beaches provided you can find a parking spot. This is not always easy in high summer. Reaching some of the beaches between Armação de Pera and Lagos involves a long or steep walk. The elderly,

disabled or lazy may wish to avoid Dona Ana, João de Arens, Vale de Currais, Paraíso, Carvalho, Marinha, Centianes, Cova, Redonda and Tramossos.

There are bars, cafes or restaurants open during the summer months at all but the smallest and more remote beaches.

From the beginning of June to the end of September many beaches have life-guards and a safety flag system. Flag colours and their meanings :
GREEN - conditions suitable for bathing and swimming
YELLOW - conditions suitable for strong swimmers only
RED - no swimming.
CHEQUERED - no life-guards on patrol.

Bibliography

A short selection of interesting reading and reference books:
ARCHITECTURE - *Churches of Portugal* by Prof. Carlos de Azevedo and Chester E.V. Brummel (Scala Books, 1985); *The Finest Churches in Portugal* by Júlio Gil and Nuno Calvet (Verbo, 1988); *The Finest Castles in Portugal* by Júlio Gil and Agusto Cabrita (Verbo, 1988)
BIRDS - *The Birds of Britain and Europe* by Hermann Heinzel, R.S.R. Fitter and John Parslow (Collins, 1972); *Birds of Southern Portugal* by Randolph Cary and Patrick Swift (privately published, 1973).
COOKING - *Traditional Portuguese Cooking* by Maria de Lourdes Modesto (Verbo, 1989).
FLORA - *Plantas do Algarve* by Maria da Luz Rocha Afonso and Mary McMurtrie (Serviço Nacional de Parques, Reservas e Conservação da Natureza, 1991).

GENERAL - *The Portuguese, the Land and its People* by Marion Kaplan (Viking 1991; Penguin, 1992).
HISTORY - *A New History of Portugal* by H. V. Livermore (Cambridge University Press, 1976); *The Portuguese Connection, the Secret History of the Azores Base* by R.E. Vintras, Bachman & Turner, 1974); *Portugal: the Last Empire* by Neil Bruce (David & Charles, 1975); *The Portuguese Seaborne Empire* 1415-1825 by C. R. Boxer (Hutchinson, 1977); *Prince Henry the Navigator* by John Ure (Constable, 1977).
TRAVEL - *Portugal's Pousada Route* by Stuart Ross (Vista Ibérica Publicações, 1992); *They Went to Portugal* by Rose Macaulay (Cape, 1946; Penguin 1985); *Algarve: a Portrait and a Guide* by David Wright and Patrick Swift (Barrie & Rockcliffe, 1965).
WINE - *Portugal's wine and Wine Makers* by Richard Mayson (Ebury Press, 1992).

Bird checklist

The following list may be useful to record the different species you have seen in southern Portugal. Some of these birds are seldom seen, but even rarer, unlisted species are probably overlooked sometimes as there are few experienced birdwatchers in the area.

... Little Grebe
... Black-necked Grebe
... Great Crested Greb
... Cory's Shearwater
... Great Shearwater
... Sooty Shearwater
... Manx Shearwater
... Gannet
... Cormorant
... Shag
... Bittern
... Night Heron
... Squacco Heron
... Cattle Egret
... Little Egret
... Grey Heron
... Purple Heron
... White Stork
... Black Stork
... Spoonbill
... Greater Flamingo
... Greylag Goose
... Shelduck
... Mallard
... Teal
... Gadwall
... Wigeon
... Pintail
... Garganey
... Shoveler
... Pochard
... Tufted Duck
... Common Scoter
... White-headed Duck
... Osprey
... Black-winged Kite
... Honey Buzzard
... Red Kite
... Black Kite
... Goshawk
... Sparrowhawk
... Buzzard

... Booted Eagle
... Bonelli's Eagle
... Imperial Eagle
... Golden Eagle
... Short-toed Eagle
... Hen Harrier
... Montagu's Harrier
... Marsh Harrier
... Egyptian Vulture
... Black Vulture
... Griffon Vulture
... Peregrine
... Hobby
... Merlin
... Lesser Kestrel
... Kestrel
... Red-legged Partridge
... Quail
... Crane
... Water Rail
... Baillon's Crake
... Moorhen
... Purple Gallinule
... Coot
... Crested Coot
... Great Bustard
... Little Bustard
... Oystercatcher
... Ringed Plover
... Little Ringed Plover
... Kentish Plover
... Golden Plover
... Grey Plover
... Lapwing
... Turnstone
... Little Stint
... Temminck's Stint
... Purple Sandpiper
... Dunlin
... Curlew Sandpiper
... Knot
... Sand Ruff

... Spotted Redshank
... Redshank
... Greenshank
... Green Sandpiper
... Common Sandpiper
... Black-tailed Godwit
... Bar-tailed Godwit
... Curlew
... Whimbrel
... Snipe
... Jack Snipe
... Black-winged Stilt
... Avocet
... Stone Curlew
... Pratincole
... Great Skua
... Pomarine Skua
... Arctic Skua
... Long-tailed Skua
... Mediterranean Gull
... Little Gull
... Black-headed Gull
... Slender-billed Gull
... Lesser Black-backed Gull
... Herring Gull
... Great Black-backed Gull
... Common Gull
... Kittiwake
... Black Tern
... Whiskered Tern
... Gull-billed Tern
... Caspian Tern
... Sandwich Tern
... Common Tern
... Arctic Tern
... Roseate Tern
... Little Tern
... Razorbill
... Guillemot
... Puffin
... Black-bellied Sandgrouse
... Pin-tailed Sandgrouse

... Wood Pigeon	...Wren	... Great Tit
... Stock Dove	...Alpine Accentor	... Nuthatch
... Rock Dove	...Dunnock	... Short-toed Tree Creeper
... Turtle Dove	...Cetti's Warbler	... Corn Bunting
... Cuckoo	...Savi's Warbler	... Yellowhammer
... Great Spotted Cuckoo	...Reed Warbler	... Rock Bunting
... Barn Owl	...Great Reed Warbler	... Ortolan Bunting
... Long-eared Owl	...Melodious Warbler	... Cirl Bunting
... Short-eared Owl	...Olivaceous Warbler	... Reed Bunting
... Scops Owl	...Orphean Warbler	... Chaffinch
... Little Owl	...Garden Warbler	... Serin
... Tawny Owl	...Blackcap	... Greenfinch
... Nightjar	...Whitethroat	... Siskin
... Red-necked Nightjar	...Sardinian Warbler	... Goldfinch
... Pallid Swift	...Subalpine Warbler	... Linnet
... Swift	...Spectacled Warbler	... Bullfinch
... Alpine Swift	...Dartford Warbler	... House Sparrow
... Kingfisher	...Willow Warbler	... Spanish Sparrow
... Bee-eater	...Chiffchaff	... Tree Sparrow
... Hoopoe	...Bonelli's Warbler	... Starling
... Roller	...Wood Warbler	... Spotless Starling
... Wryneck	...Goldcrest	... Golden Oriole
... Green Woodpecker	...Firecrest	... Jay
... Great Spotted Woodpecker	...Fan-tailed Warbler	... Azure-winged Magpie
... Lesser Spotted Woodpecker	...Pied Flycatcher	... Magpie
... Short-toed Lark	...Spotted Flycatcher	... Chough
... Lesser Short-toed Lark	...Whinchat	... Jackdaw
... Calandra Lark	...Stonechat	... Carrion Crow
... Crested Lark	...Wheatear	... Raven
... Thekla Lark	...Black-eared Wheatear	
... Wood Lark	...Rufous Bush Chat	
... Sky Lark	...Blue Rock Thrush	
... Sand Martin	...Black Redstart	
... Swallow	...Redstart	
... Red-rumped Swallow	...Robin	
... House Martin	...Nightingale	
... Crag Martin	...Bluethroat	
... Pale Crag Martin	...Fieldfare	
... Richard's Pipit	...Ring Ouzel	
... Tawny Pipit	...Blackbird	
... Tree Pipit	...Redwing	
... Meadow Pipit	...Song Thrush	
... Water / Rock Pipit	...Mistle Thrush	
... Yellow Wagtail	...Long-tailed Tit	
... Grey Wagtail	...Penduline Tit	
... White / Pied Wagtail	...Crested Tit	
... Woodchat Shrike	...Coal Tit	
... Great Grey Shrike	...Blue Tit	

Boat trips
See also: Sailing

Boat trips, long or short, give a different perspective on the Algarve's fabulous coastline.

Fishermen on many beaches offer local trips to view otherwise inaccessible sea caves and rock formations.

A morning, afternoon or whole-day cruise makes for a relaxed family outing. Whole-day trips include a cooked fish lunch and drinks on board or on a secluded beach. Cruises operate out of Vila Real de Santo António, Vilamoura, Portimão, Alvor, Lagos, Praia da Luz and Sagres. Routes and prices are advertised in tourist information offices, reception areas and on quaysides.

Motor and motor-sailing vessels are available at Vilamoura, Portimão and Lagos for more specialised day fishing and sailing trips, and for longer charters to destinations such as Lisbon, Gibraltar and Tangier.

Bowling alleys

ALBUFEIRA
Hotel Alfamar (089) 501341
ALVOR
Torralta (082) 459211
PRAIA da LUZ
Luz Bay Club (082) 789584
PRAIA DA ROCHA
beachfront road (082) 83812

Bowling greens

ALBUFEIRA
Club Praia da Oura   (089) 589135
Vale Navio   (089) 515459
VILAMOURA
Lawn Bowling Club (089) 388113

Buses

Travelling by bus in Portugal is cheap and reasonably comfortable. The main complaint is that many services are infrequent by day and do not run at all at night.

A **local and regional** bus network links all of the towns and most of the villages. It is operated by Rodoviaria Nacional (RN). All bus stations are located near town centres. Roadside stops are clearly marked with the word *paragem* in white lettering on a blue background. Fares should be paid to the driver on boarding if there is no conductor.

Express services between Vila Real de Santo António and Lagos operate twice daily in either direction stopping at a number of key places along the way. Express tickets must be bought at stations before boarding.

Lisbon and the Algarve are linked by modern, air-conditioned coaches operated by various companies - RN, Mundial Turismo, Sol, Renex and Novo Mundo. They run services from the main towns and have pick-up points at certain resorts and hotels. Travelling times vary quite a lot between services. Very roughly, Albufeira-Lisbon takes four hours; Alvor and Vilamoura-Lisbon five hours; Lagos and Vila Real de Santo António-Lisbon between five and five-and-a-half hours. **Oporto** is another four-and-a-half hours by express north of Lisbon. Tickets should be bought in advance at bus stations or agencies.

Excursions, usually half or full-day tours of the Algarve, operate regularly from several towns, resorts and hotels. Ask for details at hotel lobbies, travel agencies or tourist information offices.

Camp sites

There are more than a score of officially recognised camp sites strung out along the Algarve, part of a network of about 150 public or privately-run sites scattered throughout Portugal. All of the sites are quiet in winter and busy in summer. Standard facilities include:

* Showers; washing-up and laundry sinks.
* Electric lighting; power points for caravans and for razors.
* Self-service shopping.
* Snack bar and /or restaurant.

Some of the better camp sites have sports facilities such as tennis courts and swimming pools.

Daily prices per person, tent, car and caravan are clearly laid out and displayed.

When registering, it is necessary to leave your passport with reception until you pay your bill on leaving. Security is usually tight. In most sites only pass-holders are admitted; gates are closed to traffic at night.

Each *Parque de Turismo* is signposted with blue tent and caravan symbols on a yellow background.

Camping is not permitted on the beach or in the countryside anywhere other than at an official camp site. A cardinal rule in the countryside, particularly in summer when everything is tinder dry, is not to light fires.

Camp sites from east to west:
MONTE GORDO, 4 km west of Vila Real de Santo António. Tel. (081) 42588
CALIÇO, 2 km inland from Vila Nova de Cacela. Tel. (081) 951195
FUZETA, at the end of the village main road. Tel. (089) 793459
BANCÁRIOS, 2 km east of Olhão. Tel. (089) 705402

FARO, next to the beach, 10 km west of Faro. Tel. (089) 817876
QUARTEIRA, on east side of Quarteira. Tel. (089) 315238
ALBUFEIRA, 1.5 km short of Albufeira onhe Ferreiras road . Tel. (089) 587627
ARMAÇÃO DE PERA, just outside of town on the road from Alcantrilha Tel. (082) 312904
CANELAS, on the right-hand side of Alcantarilha-Armação road, 1 km from Alcantraliha, 1.5 km from beach. Tel. (082) 312612
FERRAGUDO, east of Ferragudo village, 4 km from Portimão. Tel. (082) 641121
PORTIMÃO, 4 km out of Portimão on the Monchique road. Tel. (082) 491012
ALVOR, on outskirts of Alvor village, 4 km from Portimão. Tel. (082) 459178
TRINIDADE, in Lagos, on the Ponta da Piedade road. Tel. (082) 763893
IMULGOS, 1.5 km from Lagos centre on the Porto de Mós road. Tel. (082) 760031
VALVERDE, 4 km from Lagos, 1.5 km short of Praia da Luz. Tel. (082) 789211
ESPICHE, 7 km west of Lagos on the N125. Tel. (082) 789431
QUINTA DOS CARRIÇOS, 16 km west of Lagos, 1 km short of Salema beach. Tel. (082) 65201
INGRINA, near the coast, 3 km south of Raposeira. Tel. (082) 66242
SAGRES, 1 km inland from Sagres village. Tel. (082) 64351
VALE DE TELHA, 6 km from Aljezur on the road to Arrifana. Tel. (082) 98444
SERRÃO, 3km north of Aljezur, on way to to Praia de Amoriera. Tel. (082) 98612
SÃO. MIGUEL, near the village of Odeceixe. Tel. (082) 94245

Car hire

International and Portuguese rental companies have offices at Faro airport and agents in all the main towns. To hire a car you must be at least 21 years old and have held a driving licence for at least one year.

The price of rental includes third party insurance. A government tax of 16% on the total is an extra which must be paid. If you choose a standard rental agreement rather than one with unlimited mileage, you will have to pay the appropriate mileage on returning the car. Optional extras: collision damage waiver, theft insurance, personal insurance.

Motor-bikes and bicycles can also be hired in many places.

Casinos

The Algarve has three casinos where you can try your luck at slot machines or play blackjack and roulette. They are open nightly from 7.0pm to 3.0am. It is essential you take along your passport. There are restaurants in the Monte Gordo and Vilamoura casinos. Vilamoura has a nightly floor-show starting at 10.30pm.

MONTE GORDO	(081)	51224/5
PRAIA DA ROCHA	(082)	23141/2
VILAMOURA	(089)	302996

Church services

Regular services are held by the Roman Catholic, Anglican, Evangelical Baptist , International Evangelical, and Dutch Protestant churches and by the Salvation army. Details of times and places can be obtained from reception desks and the local press.

The largest denomination holding Sunday services in English is the St Vincent's Anglican Church. It holds regular services in Albufeira, Almancil, Boliqueime, Penina, Praia da Luz and Santa Bárbara de Nexe, Tavira and Vilamoura. A calendar of services is published in leaflet form and distributed throughout the Algarve. The resident Chaplain may be contacted for information and in emergencies at (089) 366720.

The International Christian Fellowship holds an interdenominational service in English every Sunday morning at the Portuguese Baptist Church in Portimão.

The International Evangelical Church of the Algarve holds a service every Sunday morning at Vale Judeu.

The Dutch Protestant Church holds services every Sunday in Albufeira and Quarteira.

Cinemas

Undubbed American and British films are frequently shown in the following local cinemas:

ALBUFEIRA	Estudio Alfa
	(089) 589344
FARO	Cinema Santo António
	(089) 22238
LAGOS	Cine Teatro
	(089) 762940
LOULÉ	Cinema Charlot
	(089) 63910
OLHÃO	Cine Algarve
	(089) 713332
VILAMOURA	Vilamoura Cine
	(089) 313383

Climate

Average Air Temperatures

	Jan	Feb	Mar	Apr	May	Jun	Jul	Aug	Sep	Oct	Nov	Dec
°C	12	12	14	15	17	20	22	23	22	18	15	12
°F	53	54	57	60	63	68	72	73	70	65	59	55

* these temperatures are based on readings at the meteorology station at Faro airport, a relatively cool location. Temperatures elsewhere in the Algarve are usually warmer than these official figures suggest. Maximum daily temperatures are usually much warmer.

Average Sea Temperatures

°C	15	16	17	17	19	20	21	23	22	21	16	15
°F	60	62	62	63	67	68	70	73	72	69	62	59

Average Hours of Sunshine

177	194	207	270	325	363	395	370	296	243	178	175

Average Days of Sunshine per month

29	26	30	30	31	30	31	31	30	30	29	29

Average Annual Rainfall in mm.

	Sagres	Lagos	Praia da Rocha	Faro	Vila Real
mm	355	495	421	363	428

Consulates
See also: Embassies

Although services vary slightly between countries, broadly speaking consulates can do the following :
* Issue emergency passports
* Contact relatives and friends and ask them to help in emergencies
* Advise on how to transfer funds
* Advance a small amount of money against a cheque supported by a banker's card in real emergencies
* As a last resort and provided certain strict criteria are met, make a repayable loan for repatriation to the UK
* Provide a list of doctors, local lawyers and interpreters
* Arrange for next of kin to be informed of an accident or a death and advise on procedures
* Make contact with suspects or offenders who have been arrested or are in prison. In certain circumstances, arrange for messages to be sent to relatives or friends
* Give some guidance on organisations experienced in tracing missing persons.

Consuls generally cannot :
* Settle bills of any kind
* Pay for travel tickets
* Undertake work more properly done by staff of tour companies, airlines, banks or motoring organisations
* Give legal advice, instigate court proceedings or interfere in local judicial procedures to get foreigners out of prison
* Investigate crimes
* Help in obtaining employment.

Algarve Consulates

AUSTRIA	Praia da Rocha	(082) 416202
BELGIUM	Faro	(089) 803219
BRAZIL	Almancil	(089) 396719
BRITAIN	Portimão	(082) 417800
DENMARK	Portimão	(082) 22031
CANADA	Faro	(089) 803757
FINLAND	Faro	(089) 25482
FRANCE	Vilamoura	(089) 314475
GERMANY	Faro	(089) 803181
ICELAND	Portimão	(082) 413311
ITALY	Vila Real	(081) 44274
MEXICO	Lagos	(082) 762814
MOROCCO	Faro	(089) 27882
NETHERLANDS	Faro	(089) 20903
NORWAY	Faro	(089) 823505
SPAIN	Vila Real	(081) 44888
SWEDEN	Portimão	(082) 413311

Conversion tables

Portugal uses metric systems. The following is a guide to converting metric to British measurements and vice versa.

LINEAR MEASUREMENT:
1 metre	=	1.094 yards
1 kilometre	=	0.6214 mile
1 foot	=	0.3408 metre
1 yard	=	0.9144 metre
1 mile	=	1.609 kilometres

SQUARE MEASUREMENT:
1 square metre	=	1.196 square yards
1 hectare	=	2.471 acres
1 square yard	=	0.836 square metre
1 acre	=	0.405 hectare
1 square mile	=	259 hectares

CAPACITY MEASUREMENT:
1 litre	=	1.76 pints
1 pint	=	0.568 litre
1 gallon	=	4.546 litres

WEIGHT:
1 kilogram	=	2.205 pounds
1 ounce	=	28.35 grams
1 pound	=	0.4536 kilograms
1 stone	=	6.35 kilograms

Crime

Hard drugs have created a serious social problem in the Algarve. Heroin and the expense of maintaining its addictive use is probably the main cause behind an upsurge in bag-snatchings, theft from cars and house-breaking in recent years. While visitors should not be unduly alarmed, they should be mindful of the risks and adequately protect their belongings.

Just because you are on holiday, don't fall into the trap of ignoring the simple security precautions you would normally take at home. Take special care that cash, jewelry, cameras, and other valuables are not easy pickings.

Treat your passport, air tickets, driving licence and other documents as valuables. Although they can be replaced, it takes time and trouble which you do not need, especially when you are on holiday.

Robberies should be reported to the police. Stolen documents may turn up. Things like cameras may be retrieved, but cash almost never is.

The Portuguese police are watchful for visitors making false statements, a punishable offence, in order to submit fraudulent insurance claims when they get back home. If satisfied that your statement is genuine, however, the police will issue you with a document to hand over to your insurance company.

A person who breaks the law in Portugal cannot expect more lenient or preferential treatment just because he is a holidaymaker or a foreigner. Those arrested on suspicion of serious crime, especially offences involving violence or drugs, will find that the wheels of Portuguese justice turn slowly.

There are no foreign criminal lawyers practising in the Algarve. If you are arrested in connection with a serious offence, insist on your consulate being informed. Consular representatives can offer a certain amount of help and advice, but they cannot alter or short-circuit the judicial process.

Currency

The Portuguese currency is the *escudo*. The written abbreviation is *esc.* More commonly the $ sign is used. Not to be confused with the US dollar, the *escudo* sign is placed after the amount, not before.

Escudo notes come in denominations of 500$, 1.000$, 5.000$ and 10.000$. There are 1$, 2.50$, 5$, 10$, 20$, 50$, 100$ and 200$ coins.

A thousand *escudos* is often referred to as a *conto.* Thus 10.000 *escudos, Esc* 10.000, 10.000$ and 10 *contos* all mean the same.

Any figure after the $ sign refers to *centavos*. There are 100 *centavos* to the *escudo, but centavos* are almost valueless and nearing extinction. It is quite common and it can be quite confusion to see prices quoted thus: 10.000$00. All you have to worry about are the noughts **before** the $.

Drinks
see also: Wines

* Portuguese beer is good. It is nearly all lager, which goes with the climate, though there is a dark beer available. There is little difference between the main brands, Super Bock, Sagres and Cristal. It comes in bottles or draught. A small draught is called an *imperial.* A large one is a *caneca.* Beer of any kind is *cerveja.*
* Portuguese bar owners usually don't bother with spirit measures. Tots of whisky, brandy and so on are usually very generous compared with British tots.
* In most bars you pay when you are ready to leave as you do in a restaurant, but foreign bar owners have introduced the pay-as-you-order (*pronto pagamento*)

system. So both systems are in operation.
* Algarve-produced wine comes in 1.5 litre and five litre returnable bottles. Be warned that if you drink too much of it too quickly you will suffer; if you do not drink it quickly enough and leave it standing open for a several days it will become undrinkable.
* It is not disreputable to add lemonade-type soft drinks to soften or sweeten the taste of cheap wines. The locals do it sometimes, so that makes it okay. However, it is unthinkable to dilute or adulterate in any way wines with the word *reserva* or *garrafeira* on the label for these words denote a wine of distinction.
* Some Portuguese or Algarvean alcoholic specialities: White Port is a dry aperitif; *Amêndoa Amarga* (almond) *Brandy Mel* (honey) and *Licor Beirão* (aromatic plants) are liqueurs. *Medronho* (arbutus berries) *figo* (from figs) and *bagaceira* (from grape husks) are ardent spirits, ie firewaters.
* Some Ports are better than others, but all are good. All genuine Ports - white, red, tawny, vintage character, vintage and LBV - carry the Port Wine Institute's seal. The reds and rubies are young, sweet and fruity. The tawnies are semi-sweet or sweet and usually older than the reds. The very good ones are labelled with an indication of their age: 10, 20, 30 or 40 years. True vintage Port is the unblended product of a single harvest of outstanding or rare quality. LBV (late bottled vintage) Ports stand in oak casks for between four and six years before bottling. Prices depend on quality. The best may cost an arm and a leg, but perfectly good Ports can be bought for a modest amount of money.
* Mineral water comes in 1.5 litre and five litre bottles. The glass five litre glass bottles are returnable.

Approximate distances by road

```
                                                      Albufeira
                                                Aljezur  81
                                          Almancil  97  26
                                            Alvor  53  49  37
                               Armação de Pera  25  34  66  18
                                       Faro  47  66  13 110  39
                                 Lagoa  54  13  12  41  56  25
                            Lagos  26  80  39  19  67  30  51
                      Loulé  68  42  16  35  54   8  98  27
               Monchique  75  41  33  87  46  29  74  71  58
                 Olhão  95  24  88  62   9  55  74  21 118  47
            Portimão  70  25  50  18   8  62  21   4  40  25  33
          Quarteira  52  30  77  11  70  44  22  37  56   9 100  29
            Sagres 102  63 120  73 100  32  58 112  71  51  99  42  83
S. Bart. de Messines  83  35  33  53  58  33  51  36  45  29  37  32  81  21
 S. Brás de Alportel  46 113  24  63  17  88  13  81  55  17  48  67  21 111  40
             Silves  63  17  66  52  16  70  41  50  34   8  62  21  20  43  64  33
             Tavira  85  22  68 135  46  85  20 110  35 103  77  29  70  89  43 133  62
          Vila Real  23 108  45  91 158  69 108  43 133  58 126 100  52  93 112  66 150  85
```

Driving

Some points to bear in mind :
* Drive on the right-hand side of the road.
* Seat belts must be worn in the front seats, and in the back if fitted.
* Under 13-year-olds must not travel in the front seats.
* Speed limits: 60 kph (37 mph) in built up area, 90 kph (56 mph) on the open road
* Give way to the right where roads of equal importance meet.
* The general standard of driving in the Algarve is appalling. The accident rate is amongst the highest in Europe.
* The roads are getting better, but many remain unsurfaced,   badly pot-holed or with dangerously ragged edges.
* Spot checks on vehicles are common. Make sure you have your documents at hand, including a valid driving licence and appropriate insurance.
* Do not assume that because you are a visitor the police will look lightly or turn a blind eye on traffic infringements. They won't. On-the-spot fines may be imposed
* The drink-driving laws here carry very stiff penalties. You may be stopped at any time and asked to undergo a breathalyser test.
* If you are involved in an accident, exchange insurance details. It there is injury or serious damage, ask someone to phone the police. The nationwide phone number for the police and ambulance is 115.
*   Petrol stations are fairly plentiful along the south coastal strip, but scarcer on the west coast and the further inland you go. Most filling stations sell leaded and unleaded super, normal petrol, and diesel fuel. Compared with most other European countries, petrol is expensive here.

Eating in

BUYING FOOD

Visitors on self-catering holidays will find shopping for food much the same as elsewhere in Europe though naturally there are some regional peculiarities. While a few large shopping centres have sprung up and various sizes of supermarket abound, the old-fashioned town and village market-place still flourishes. Meat, fish, fruit and vegetables can be bought fresh at public markets each morning except Sundays and public holidays. Prices in the market-place are generally much cheaper than in shops

Chicken is excellent. Of the other **meats,** pork is probably the most consistently good. Beef, lamb, kid, turkey and duck are all usually available; sometimes you can buy rabbit and quail.

An abundance and wide variety of **seafood** arrives at markets straight from the sea. The day's prices are written up on blackboards by the market stalls. If they are not too busy, most fishmongers will be glad to de-gut and scale fish for you while you wait.

The Algarve, called by some ''the garden of Portugal,'' has a great array of home-grown **vegetables and fruits.** Broad beans, lettuce, cabbage, cauliflower, aubergines, sweet potatoes, tomatoes, cucumbers and courgettes are all plentiful, but only in their season. The same is true of grapes, olives, figs, peaches, plums, nectarines, cherries and more exotic pomegranates, loquats and kiwi fruits.

The Portuguese are particularly fond of onions, tomatoes and garlic mixed in oil and vinegar with lots of chopped parsley and freshly-ground black pepper.

Refined and cellophane-wrapped **bread**

is on sale in some supermarkets, but the best and most popular bread is still the traditional white rolls (*papessecos*) and three types of loaf - light, crusty white, heavier white and wholemeal.

Cheese falls into four main types : *Ilha* from the Azores is similar to cheddar; *serra* is a soft, mild-tasting goat's cheese; Portugal also makes Edam-like cheeses and very tasty Camembert.

Fresh **milk** packaged in awkward sachets is sold in some supermarkets, but most milk is of the "long life" type which comes in cardboard cartons or plastic bottles in three grades - normal (*gordo*), low-fat (*meio gordo*) and skimmed (*magro*).

COOKING

The story is told of the old man who went begging for food from door to door. He was poor but proud. Rather than admit he had nothing at all to put in his pot, he said he had a stone but needed something to go with it. The first person he asked gave a potato, the second a carrot and so on until he had the ingredients for a wholesome soup. In the Algarve they still call this kind of hotchpotch *sopa de pedra,* meaning "soup of the stone." Here are some other typical and fairly easy regional recipes:

Shredded Cabbage Soup / *Caldo Verde*
   750g potatoes
   250g finely shredded cabbage
   2 onions
   5 tbsp olive oil
   salt
Boil peeled, cut up potatoes with roughly chopped onion together with salt and 2 tbsp of olive oil. When soft, puree or mash with a fork. Return to the pan and bring to the boil again. Add the washed, shredded cabbage which can be bought by the kilo already shredded in any vegetable market. Leave to cook for 10 minutes. It is traditional to serve in a bowl with a little more olive oil or thin slices of red *chouriço* sausage added. Serves 4.

Fish, Lamb or Kid Stew
Caldeirada de Peixe* or *de Cabrito

1.5 kg mixed fish, such as sea bass, sea bream, dogfish, sardines or other fish with few awkward bones. Alternatively, 1.5 kg lamb or kid. Also:
750g potatoes
3 green peppers
1 kg tomatoes
3 onions
bunch of parsley
piri-piri sauce
salt
3 cloves garlic
3 bay leaves
4 heads of cloves
   Cut fish into cutlets or leave whole if not too large. (Trim the meat, which should be from the neck, breast or chops). Peel and slice vegetables. Place alternate layers of vegetables and fish or meat; season and continue until all the ingredients have been used up. End with a layer of potato and add a spoon of olive oil and butter (plus a glass of white wine if you wish). Cook over a low heat with a tight-fitting lid for about 45 minutes.

   To make a special *caldeirada de peixe,* add 500g of well-washed cockles or clams 10 minutes before the stew is ready. Meat *caldeirada* is usually quite spicy, but extra piri-piri can be added separately. To decorate, use plenty of parsley and a grated lemon rind. Serves 4.

Stewed Shellfish
Cataplana
1.5 kg clams or mussels
4 slices bacon
6 cloves of garlic
a quarter of red *chouriço* sausage
few drops piri-piri sauce
salt & pepper
parsley
1 tbsp olive oil

This dish takes its Portuguese name from the enclosed vessel it is cooked in. It is a clam-shaped frying pan with a tight fitting lid. These pans can be bought either in beaten copper or much cheaper metal alloy versions.

Soak the shellfish overnight in a bowl of water with a handful of rough salt. Rinse well. Heat olive oil in the pan and add finely chopped onion. Fry lightly then add chopped bacon, garlic, *chouriço*, parsley and shellfish and season with piri-piri, salt and pepper.

Close the lid tightly and cook on a gas flame for 10 minutes. Turn over and cook for another 10 minutes. Open the *cataplana* pan with the hinged side facing up and serve. Serves 4.

Salted Cod à Brás
Bacalhau à Brás
400g dried, salted cod
500 kg potatoes
6 eggs
3 onions
parsley
4 cloves garlic
3 tbsp olive oil
salt & pepper
cooking oil
a few black olives

Soak strips of cod for 24 hours in fresh water which should be changed several times. The fish is then ready for cooking in any one of 365 different ways, or so it is said in Portugal. This is one way which foreigners seem to like very much:

Shred the potatoes or make very small chips. Slice the onions and chop the garlic. Remove the skin and bones from the fish. Flake into pieces.

Fry the potatoes in cooking oil until brown. Drain on absorbent paper. Gently fry onions and garlic in olive oil in a thick casserole. Shred the cod and add to the pan stirring with a wooden spoon. Add the fried potatoes.

Beat the eggs and pour them over the cod and potatoes. Stir the eggs with a fork until the mixture is creamy. Serve hot with chopped parsley and olives. Serves 4.

Eating out
see also: the reverse side of the *Insider's Tourist Map of the Algarve.*

* The only problem with eating out is choosing where, the choice being very extensive. Restaurants are officially rated from third class to *de luxo,* but these ratings refer to the quality of the premises and facilities, not the quality of the food and the service.

* Menus are usually displayed outside restaurants, so you can check on prices and what's on offer before you commit yourself to a table. For a fair idea of how cheap or expensive a restaurant is, you usually need look no further than the price of the soups.

* The most reliable recommendation for a restaurant is that of someone unconnected to it who has eaten there recently. In tourist areas, the turnover of owners, managers

and chefs is high, which means that standards in any one establishment may suddenly fluctuate.

* Restaurants are obliged to offer a set "tourist menu" (*menu de turista*), which should be reasonably priced. Check also if there is a "dish of the day"(*prato do dia*). It is likely to be served with little delay and will probably be fresher and cheaper than other dishes.

* When the menu shows a variable price marked P.V.(meaning *preço variável*), it must also show the price per kilo of the food concerned.

* The prices you pay for drinks or dishes should be the same as those displayed. All taxes and service charges are included. Tips should be added if appropriate. Between 5% and 10% is about right for satisfactory service.

* Menus are supposed to show the price and composition of the *couvert* (bread and butter, perhaps fresh cheese and olives). It may be automatically served, but if you do not want it, send it back and you are not obliged to pay for it.

* If you feel you have grounds for complaint, ask for the manager. If you receive no satisfaction from the manager, ask for the official complaints book. All restaurants are supposed to keep one. If you lodge a complaint, or intend to later, make sure you get a detailed receipt for the meal.

Electricity

220 volts AC with continental two-pin plugs is the norm. Considerable fluctuations in voltage occur in some areas. Sudden cuts in the supply are not unusual, especially when there is heavy rain.

Some Portuguese menu meanings:

Amêijoas - clams
Arroz de marisco - shellfish rice.
Arroz doce - rice pudding with cinnamon.
Bacalhau - salted cod
Batatas cozidas - boiled potatoes
Batatas fritas - chips
Bife de vaca - beef steak
Bife de vitela - veal steak
Caldo verde - potato-based cabbage soup.
Caldeirada de cabrito - lamb or kid stew.
Carne - meat.
Cataplana - steamed pork with clams.
Costeletas de porco - pork chops.
Espetada - kebab.
Entrecosto - spare ribs.
Febras de porco - loin of pork.
Feijoada - pork and bean stew.
Frango assado - grilled chicken.
Gambas - prawns
Jardineira - beef and vegetable stew.
Legumes - vegetables.
Leitão - suckling pig.
Lombo de porco - pork filet.
Lulas recheadas - stuffed squid.
Pato - duck
Peixe - fish.
Perú - turkey.
Sobremesa - dessert
Sopa - soup.
Tarte de natas - cream cake

Cooking terms:
Assado - roasted.
Cozido - boiled.
Estufado - braised.
Grelhado - grilled.
Na brasa - charcoal grilled
No forno - baked.
Bem passado - well done.
Mal pessado - rare or underdone.

Embassies
See also: Consulates

Several countries whose nationals are frequent visitors to the Algarve do not maintain consulates in the province. In such cases, difficulties should be referred to the consular section of the appropriate Embassy in Lisbon :

For Lisbon, first dial 01 ...

AUSTRALIAN	523350
IRISH	661569
ITALIAN	546144
SOUTH AFRICAN	535041
UNITED STATES	726660

Emergencies

URGENT HELP

When phoning, seek the help of someone who speaks Portuguese if possible because emergency service personnel often do not understand English.

Anywhere in Portugal, **dial 115** without charge and ask the operator for police (*polícia*) ambulance (*ambulância*) or fire services (*bombeiros*).

	LOCAL POLICE	FIRE / AMBULANCE
ALBUFEIRA	(089) 512205	(089) 586333
ALCANTARILHA	(082) 322210	(082) 442411
ALJEZUR	(082) 98130	(082) 98258
ARMAÇÃO	(082) 322210	(082) 442411
CARVOEIRO	(082) 356460	(082) 52888
FARO	(089) 803444	(089) 822122
LAGOA	(082) 52310	(082) 52888
LAGOS	(082) 762809	(082) 760115
LOULÉ	(082) 62782	(089) 416702
MONCHIQUE	(082) 92629	(082) 92529
OLHÃO	(089) 703089	(089) 704994
PORTIMÃO	(082) 417217	(082) 22122
QUARTEIRA	(089) 315662	(089) 314589
SÃO BRÁS	(089) 842210	(089) 842666
TAVIRA	(081) 22417	(081) 22123
VILA DO BISPO	(082) 66112	(082) 66285
VILA REAL	(081) 44355	(081) 43202

ILLNESS OR INJURY

There are English-speaking private doctors and dentists with surgeries or clinics within easy reach of most places along the south coast.

Treatment is also available to visitors at any of the three state-run hospitals, which are open 24-hours a day:

Faro   (089) 803411
Portimão   (082) 415115
Lagos   (082) 763034

DEATH

In the event of the death in the Algarve of a relative or friend, immediately contact your consulate here or the consular section of your embassy in Lisbon. They will be able to help you make all the necessary arrangements.

Festivals

Spring

INTERNATIONAL ALMOND BLOSSOM CROSS COUNTRY RACE held in conjunction with the European Cross Country Club Champions Championship is an athletics meeting with a festive atmosphere. It attracts many of Europe's best long-distance runners and many spectators. Aldeia das Açoteias, between Albufeira and Vilamoura, is the venue. It is held each **January.**

THE NATIONAL ORANGE FESTIVAL at Silves is an agricultural trade fair featuring everything connected with citrus production. **February.**

CARNIVAL is when people either come out to watch the processions of floats and join in all the drinking, dancing and fancy dress fun, or they well clear of all the revelry. Loulé is the main centre of carnival activity. Long weekend **before Lent.**

THE ALGARVE INTERNATIONAL MUSIC FESTIVAL, though modest compared with Europe's better known music festivals, grows in stature each year with performances in various parts of the province by high-calibre exponents of classical music and ballet. **April, May and June.**

THE ROMARIA DE SENHORA DA PIEDADE, or more simply the Mãe Soberana celebrations, centre on the image of the Virgin Mary which is taken in procession from a shrine near Loulé and returned there a week later. **Easter.**

THE FIRST OF MAY festivities in Alte bring out all the local folklore traditions and feature a colourful procession to the village's Fonte Grande in celebration of water, the symbol of life.

Summer

SILVES BEER FESTIVAL provides an opportunity to compare the various Portuguese brews within the floodlit walls of the castle while live bands play music for listening and dancing. **July.**

FEIRA DA SENHORA DO CARMO in Faro is the region's foremost agricultural fair which increasingly features consumer goods along with handicrafts and entertainment. **July.**

FATACIL in Lagoa is the Western Algarve's biggest outdoor trade fair. It has developed into a fairly slick showplace for all manner of handicrafts, agricultural and domestic products. **August.**

A SHELLFISH FESTIVAL brings congenial crowds to eat seafood and drink wine in the region's premier fishing port of Olhão. **August**
THE FESTA E FEIRA DA SENHORA DOS MARTIRES combines celebrations in honour of "Our Lady of the Martyrs" with a country fair in the lovely setting of Castro Marim in the extreme east of the Algarve. **August.**
THE ALGARVE FOLK MUSIC AND DANCE FESTIVAL culminates on Praia da Rocha beach with the grand final of a competition which brings together groups in regional costume from all over Portugal. **September.**

Autumn

THE ALGARVE INTERNATIONAL DOG SHOW has a wide and faithful following of breeders and spectators who turn up each year at Aldeia das Açoteias, between Albufeira and Vilamoura, to see Portuguese and many exotic breeds compete under international rules. **October.**

Golf courses

Although golf is an all-year-round sport in southern Portugal, conditions are best from November to April.

The design and the degree of challenge offered by each of the 16 courses in the Algarve vary considerably, but there are courses suitable for everyone from high-handicap novices to professionals.

Most courses are open to visitors for the price of a green fee. A few are restricted to property owners in associated developments or guests at specific hotels.

Others give priority, but not exclusivity, to such players.

Each of the Algarve's golf club's has a resident professional; most include among their facilities a pro shop, buggies, trolleys and clubs for hire, a driving range and practise green. The established courses from east to west :
SAN LORENZO - An exquisite 18-hole par 72 championship course on the Quinta do Lago development 15 km west of Faro airport. It is located among pines and lakes bordering the Ria Formosa nature reserve. It is for the exclusive use of guests staying at the Dona Filipa and Penina hotels. Tel. (089) 396522.
QUINTA DO LAGO - Four integrated 9-hole courses on the Quinta do Lago development offer options for 9 and 18-hole play. The scene of many Portuguese Open and other big tournaments, this is rated by many, including top professionals, as one of the best golf complexes in Europe. Tel. (089) 394529 or 394782.
PINHEIROS ALTOS - Situated amid 250 acres of pine woods in the north-east corner of the Quinta do Lago estate, this is one of the Algarve's newest 18-hole golf courses. The first 9 holes were inaugurated in June 1992 by the 1992 British Masters winner, Christy O'Connor Jr. Tel. (089) 398194.
VALE DO LOBO - The three 9-hole loops on the Vale do Lobo development 20 km west of Faro airport were designed by Henry Cotton. The fairly narrow fairways undulate through pine trees close to a spectacular stretch of coastline. The 7th on the Yellow Course straddles two ravines and is reputed to be Europe's most photographed hole. Tel. (089) 393939.
VILA SOL - An American-style 18-hole course opened in early 1990 on a new golf

complex 20 minutes by car from Faro. It is 6,183 metres long and laid out on gentle, naturally rolling countryside. Most of the tees and greens are elevated and the fairways are through avenues of umbrella pines. Tel. (089) 302144.

VILAMOURA I - An English-style championship course of 18 holes, the first of three courses built on the huge Vilamoura estate 25 km west of Faro airport. The setting is gentle, pine-covered slopes near the sea. Players on this and the other two Vilamoura courses must produce handicap certificates. Tel. (089) 313652.

VILAMOURA II - A lovely 18-hole par 72 course in two contrasting halves, the first open and in view of the sea, the second rising through pine trees. Its relatively small greens are a good test of accuracy. Several holes were reconstructed by the American architect Robert Trent Jones to improve the old Dom Pedro course's playability and popularity. Tel. (089) 315562.

VILAMOURA III - Three 9-hole loops through pine parkland and among lakes. A major renovation programme expected to be completed in autumn 1993. Tel. (089) 887022.

PINE CLIFFS - Nine spectacular holes along the clifftops above one of the region's loveliest beaches. A compact course for the exclusive use of owners and guests of the Pine Cliffs Golf and Country Club, and the Sheraton Hotel. Tel. (089) 501785.

VALE DO MINHO - Nine holes, each a par 3, in the Jorge de Lagos Golf Village just east of Carvoeiro, about an hour's drive from Faro. It is especially designed for holiday golfers; a good test of precision play. Tel. (082) 358502.

QUINTA DO GRAMACHO - A double 9-hole course, the first of its kind in continental Europe, just west of Carvoeiro. It is associated with the Euroactividade (Carvoeiro Club) group of developments. There are 18 sets of tees and greens which offer two separate 9-hole rounds through attractive, easy-to-walk countryside. Tel. (082) 341663.

VALE DA PINTA - Euroactividade's second Carvoeiro course is over 18 holes with a par of 71 and measuring 5,828 metres. Ancient olive trees have been carefully conserved and are integrated with groves of almond and fig trees throughout the lovely rolling terrain. The Algarve's newest golf course; it opened at the end of 1992. Tel. (082) 341663.

ALTO GOLF - An 18-hole championship-length course for holidaying players of all standards. Located near Alvor just west of Portimão, it is laid out on farmland formerly devoted to the cultivation of figs and olives. Its most memorable hole, "Henry Cotton's challenge," is one of the longest in Europe at 604 metres. Tel. (082) 416913.

PENINA - Laid out in 1966 in the grounds of the venerable, five-star Penina Hotel 5 km west of Portimão, this is the Algarve's oldest golf course and the first to be designed by the late Sir Henry Cotton. The flat, 18-hole championship course is supplemented by two 9-hole courses among eucalyptus trees. Tel. (982) 415415.

PALMARES - A scenic 18-hole par 71 course a few kilometres east of Lagos with views of Lagos Bay in front and the Monchique mountains behind. Five of the holes are on sand dunes next to the beach. The rest are through undulating parkland strewn with almond trees, which means its broad fairways are at their loveliest in January and February. Tel. (082) 762961. PARQUE DA FLORESTA - The Algarve's most westerly course is both dramatic and demanding. The first of its 18 holes is across a chasm and measures 564 metres. Situated about 16 km west of Lagos and near the village of Budens, the terrain is hilly. You will probably want the help of a buggy to get around. Tel. (082) 65333.

PORTIMÃO
Centro Hipico da Penina   (082) 415415
Vale de Ferro (Mexilhoeira Grande)
                          (082) 96444

SAGRES
Centro Hipico de Sagres   (082) 64212

VILAMOURA
Centro Hipico   (089) 322675

Horse-riding

There are facilities at various places for beginners as well as experienced riders interested in hacking, dressage and jumping. Individual and group lessons are available. Riding stables, listed under the nearest town, are located as follows:

ALBUFEIRA	Tel.
Aldeia das Açoteias	(089) 501267
Alfamar	(089) 501351
Quinta da Balaia	(089) 586575
Quinta da Saudade (Guia)	(089) 5919782
Vale Navio	(089) 515459

ALMANCIL
Horses' Paradise   (089) 396864
Pinetrees Riding Centre
(Quinta do Lago)   (089) 396902

LAGOA
Casa Agricola Solear (Porches)
                          (082) 52406

LAGOS
West Algarve Riding Centre (Burgau)
                          (082) 69152
Tiffany's Riding Centre (Espiche)
                          (089) 65395

Markets

In addition to municipal food markets, travelling markets do the rounds. They are called "regional" markets and they sweep into town overnight. Stalls are set up, may of them by Gypsies, to sell clothes, shoes, household goods of various kinds and all manner of bric-a-brac. They spend at least one day per month in each town and major village:

ALBUFEIRA	First and Third Tuesday
ALTE	Third Thursday
ALJEZUR	Third Monday
ARMAÇÃO DE PERA	First Thursday

(October to March)   First Sunday (April and May) First and Third Sunday (June to September)

BENSAFRIM	Second Monday
CACHOPO	First Saturday
ESTÓI	Second Sunday
FUSETA	First Thursday
LAGOA	Second Sunday (except July and August)
LAGOS	First Saturday
LOULÉ	Every Saturday
MESSINES	Fourth Monday
MONCARAPACHO	First Sunday

MONCHIQUE	Second Friday
ODEÁXERE	Fourth Monday
PORTIMÃO	First Monday
QUARTEIRA	Every Wednesday
ROGIL	Second Monday
SAGRES	Every Friday
S. BRÁS	Every Saturday
S. MARCOS	First Monday
SILVES	Third Monday
TAVIRA	Third Monday
VILA REAL	Third Sunday

Museums

FARO

ARCHAEOLOGICAL MUSEUM, Praça Afonso III: archaeological artefacts, including ceramics, sculpture, paintings, jewelry, coins and medals. Open 0900 - 1200 hrs and 1400 - 1700 hrs daily except Saturday, Sunday and public holidays. Tel. (089) 822042 ext. 236

MUSEUM OF REGIONAL ETHNOLOGY, Praça da Liberdade: artefacts, models and displays of traditional rural life in the Algarve. Open 8.30am - 12.30pm and 2.0pm - 5.0pm daily except Saturday, Sunday and public holidays. Tel. (089) 27610

MARITIME MUSEUM, Port Captain's building near the Eva Hotel: model boats and other displays. Open 10.0am - 11.0am and 2.30pm - 4.30pm weekdays, 9.30am - 1.0pm Saturday. Closed Sunday and public holidays. Tel. (089) 803601.

LAGOS

LAGOS REGIONAL MUSEUM, Rua General Alberto Carlos da Silveira, next to church of Santo António: archaeological artefacts, ethnological displays, painting and religious works of art. Open 0930 - 1230 hrs and 1400 - 1700 hrs daily except Monday and public holidays. Tel. (082) 762301

SILVES

SILVES ARCHAEOLOGICAL MUSEUM, Rua das Portas de Loulé: A Moorish well and displays of various ancient and medieval artefacts. Open 10.0am - 12.30pm and 2.30pm - 6.0pm daily except public holidays. Tel. (082) 444832

TAVIRA

MONTE DA GUERREIRA MUSEUM, Monte da Guerreira, Santo Estevão: furniture, silverware, crystal, ceramics and religious art. A private museum open daily. Tel. (081) 961179

VILAMOURA

VILAMOURA ROMAN RUINS, near the marina: Roman and Moorish artefacts on the site where they were excavated. Open 10.0am - 5.0pm daily in winter; 1000 - 2000 hrs daily in summer. Tel: (089) 32153

VILA REAL DE SANTO ANTÓNIO

MANUEL CABANAS NATIONAL GALLERY, Praça Marques de Pombal: lithographs, wood carvings, traditional regional costumes. Open 11.30am - 12.30pm and 2.0pm - 7.0pm daily except Monday and public holidays. Tel. (081) 43030

Newspapers

There are two English-language weeklies (APN and Algarve Resident) and a fortnightly (Algarve News). Many foreign dailies are available, but most only arrive on the newsstands a day after publication.

Pests

MOSQUITOES

Public nuisance number one. Though they do not spread disease, their bite is irritating. Numbers fluctuate greatly, but they are around all summer. Although most active at sunset, they stay busy all night.

If you are under attack outdoors, apply a liquid or cream repellent to exposed parts. Indoors, zap them with any suitable swat or fumigate with "Dum Dum" or similar insecticide spray. For trouble-free sleep, plug a "Baygon" electric diffuser unit into a wall socket in the bedroom. The rechargeable tablets deter mosquitoes for eighteen hours, even with the lights on and the windows open, according to the manufacturers.

If your defences are breached and you get bitten, a little "Fenergan" cream rubbed on the spot soon takes away the itch and the swelling.

ANTS

They are only a nuisance during those unpredictable days in high summer when they decide to swarm indoors in regimented lines in search of carelessly discarded or uncovered food. Normally they eat other insects. A general insecticide spray will kill ants in the house. Otherwise, they can simply be wiped or brushed away. Points of entry, such as cracks in the walls or gaps by windows and doors should be powdered with "Mata Formigas" or a similar anti-ant product.

TICKS

The least common, but potentially the most troublesome of the creepy-crawly pests. They are very small, parasitic mites which attach themselves to hosts by burying their head in the skin. They are blood-suckers and the female of some species inflate like big, grey warts of blood. Dogs often get ticks. Humans may pick them up from dogs or while walking through tick-infested countryside. Humans are liable to contract tick fever which requires urgent medical treatment. The symptoms are a loss of appetite, high temperature and a blotchy rash.

Ticks should be removed from the skin of animals or humans with a pair of tweezers rather than with the fingers, to ensure that the parasite's head is not left embedded. They can be encouraged to let go by dabbing them with pure alcohol. Drop them into kerosene or boiling water.

Postal services

Post offices are generally open from 8.30 am to 6.0pm on weekdays, closed Saturdays, Sundays and public holidays. In small towns and villages they close for lunch. The service is reliable, but the speed of delivery both within Portugal and to overseas destinations has the reputation of being rather slow and erratic. Count on 10 days for a letter or card to reach Britain, Germany or elsewhere in northern Europe.

District postal codes :

Albufeira	8200
Almancil	8135
Armação de Pera	8365
Faro	8000
Loulé	8100
Lagos	8600
Lagoa	8400
Monchique	8550
Olhão	8700
Portimão	8500

Silves	8300
Tavira	8800
Vila Real	8900

Public Holidays

Banks, post offices and government offices close on national and local public holidays. So do many, but not all shops. Some bus services are curtailed. Maids looking after self-catering accommodation take the day off. Otherwise, as far as visitors are concerned, business is pretty much as usual.

National Holidays:

January 1	New Year's Day
March / April	Good Friday
May 1	Revolution Day
May / June	Corpus Christi
June 10	Camões Day
August 15	Ascension Day
October 5	Republic Day
November 1	All Saints' Day
December 1	Independence Day
December 8	Immaculate Conception
December 25	Christmas Day

Local Holidays

April 1	Monchique
May 13	Vila Real de Santo António
June 1	São Brás de Alportel
June 16	Olhão
June 24	Castro Marim, Faro, & Tavira
August 20	Albufeira & Loulé
August 29	Aljezur
September 3	Silves
September 8	Lagoa
September 9	Alcoutim
September 20	Vila do Bispo
September 27	Lagos
December 11	Portimão

Radio and TV

Many Portuguese local and national stations can be picked up on ordinary portable radios. The best FM stations for pop music with information and news slots in English: 94MHz (Albufeira), 101.2 (Albufeira) and 104 (Lagos). The best frequency for classical music: 91.6 MHz.

A short wave receiver is needed to pick up English-language programmes on the World Service of the BBC. The best frequencies: MHz 9.410, 9.670, 12.095, 15.070 or 21.710. In the early morning and late at night, lower frequencies are usually best.

The World Service broadcasts news on the hour every hour. Financial news is at 2230 hrs GMT Mondays to Fridays, repeated 0445 hrs and 0930 hrs GMT Tuesdays to Saturdays.

Stock market reports are at 1939 hrs GMT on weekdays. Saturday sport, with live commentaries on major sporting events in Britain, starts at 1345 hrs or 1400 hrs GMT.

There are four Portuguese commercial television channels, Canal 1, TV2, SIC and Canal 4. They often show English-language films, drama series, soap operas and documentaries and spectacular international events. TV2 in particular also screens live coverage of major international sports events, such as Forumula One racing, and recordings of various other competitions including Five Nations rugby internationals.

Many hotels and tourist complexes have receiving equipment for satellite TV channels such as Sky News, CNN and Eurosport.

Sailing

Days along the Algarve coast typically begin with little wind and flat water. These conditions prevail throughout the morning. The wind normally freshens in the afternoon. It can come up suddenly or dramatically change direction very quickly. This can cause problems for inexperienced sailors. The prevailing summer wind comes from the north-west and this provides good conditions for sailing. Southerlies and the "Levanter" east wind whip up big waves and often keeps local fishing boats in the harbours.

Official ports of entry for yachtsmen (east to west): Vila Real de Santo António, Olhão, Faro, Vilamoura, and Olhão. Faro and Olhão are best entered on a rising tide because of currents of up to 5 knots when the tide is falling. There is good mooring at Sagres and within the moles at Portimão. Mooring is free of charge at all of the harbours except Vilamoura, which is the only place along the Algarve coast with a marina and comprehensive facilities for yachts, and Lagos, which is expected to have a new marina at the end of 1993.

South-easterlies can be bad news, south-westerlies even worse, when they blow upwards of 25 knots with accompanying big swells. Under such conditions, all of the Algarve's ports sometimes officially close, or it may be unwise to try to enter them. The best option may be to shelter on the west side of the Cape St Vincent lighthouse.

Because of licensing regulations in Portugal, there are no "bare boats" for hire, though it may be possible to hire a boat with a skipper. Sailing dinghies and small catamarans, however, can be hired easily at a number of places, including Pedras d'el Rei near Tavira, Vilamoura, Ferragudo, Lagos, Praia da Luz and Burgau.

Scuba-diving

Weather permitting, scuba-diving is an all-year-round sport off the western half of the south coast. where there are reefs, abundant marine life and a number of wrecks in 20 metres or so of water.

Diving centres offer courses for beginners and right up to advanced levels. They hire equipment and arrange offshore trips for experienced divers.

From east to west:
ATLANTIC DIVING CENTRE, Aveiros Beach, Albufeira, Tel. (089) 587479, is the official agent in the Algarve for the British Sub-Aqua Club and associated with PADI.

ALGARVE DIVING CENTRE, Praia Senhora da Rocha, Armação de Pera, Tel. (082) 313989, is also associated with the international organisation PADI.

THE SEASPORTS CENTRE, Praia da Luz, Tel. (082) 789538, is a member of the European federation of sub-aqua associations, CMAS.

Shooting (clay pigeon)

The main centre is at Vilamoura, Tel. (089) 302545. Equipment and facilities are available for skeet, sporting and Olympic trap shooting. It is open all-year-round. Summer hours: 10.0am - 1.0pm, 3.30pm - 8.0pm. Winter hours: 9.30am - 1.0pm, 2.0pm - 6.0pm. Competitions are usually held at weekends.

Shopping

* Every town has a general shopping area with items most visitors are likely to need. Prices are set and generally marked. Little haggling goes on except at regional markets.
* Opening is usually 9.30am. Closing is normally 7.0pm. The lunch break is commonly for two hours from 1.0pm. Most shops close Saturday afternoon and Sunday. Certain shopping centres in Albufeira and Portimão stay open late every night.
* Fresh foodstuffs are cheapest at municipal markets most of which open daily, except Sundays, mornings only.
* Faro and Portimão are by far the biggest shopping centres with a better range of merchandise than anywhere else, but places like Loulé and Monchique are good for shopping because they specialise in traditional goods and items made by craftsmen.
* Good regional buys:
LEATHER - Shoes by top designers with high quality workmanship; handbags, purses, belts and slippers.
CORK - Table mats and carved ornaments.
POTTERY - Large selection of colourful, hand painted plates, pots and vases.
TABLE-CLOTHS - Hand-embroidered in all shapes and sizes, but beware of imitations being offered as the real thing.
COPPERWARE - Go for the better quality work.
GOLD & SILVER - Filigree work is of a generally good standard and inexpensive.

Snorkelling

The sandy-bottomed eastern half of the south coast is not nearly as interesting as the western half which has wonderful underwater rock formations which attract a wide variety of fish. Just off Praia da Marinha, east of Carvoeiro, and Ponta da Piedade, west of Lagos, are examples of good snorkeling grounds.

Sunshine and calm seas are the main ingredients to ensure good visibility. These conditions may be found at any time of the year. The safest and most rewarding time of the day to snorkel is when the tiding is coming in. Beware particularly of the outgoing tide on the west coast where the undertow is strong.

The chilly waters of the Atlantic make it necessary to wear a wet suit for nine months of the year. The only months a wet suit is not essential are July, August and September.

If you want to spear fish, you must buy a temporary fishing licence from a Port Captain's office. When fishing, it is important you mark your whereabouts in the water with a red or pink buoy. Failure to do this may result in a court fine or a confrontation with a passing speedboat.

All the necessary gear for snorkeling can be bought locally.

Surfing
See also: Windsurfing

Of the fairly centrally located, popular beaches, the best for surfing is Praia da Rocha. Otherwise, to find good waves you have to go to the Algarve's south-west corner, especially to Zavial, about 5 km south of Raposeira, Tonel, on the west side of the Sagres headland, and to Ponta Ruiva and Cordama on the West Coast near Vila do Bispo. The good thing about the twin promontories of Sagres and Cape St Vincent is that you can usually find rollers on one side or the other, whichever way the wind is blowing. Don't forget the undertow!

Taxis

* Easily recognised: they are painted black with green roofs.
* Fares from the airport to all towns and resorts are set. Establish the listed price before you start off. Fares for other trips are according to the meter.
* There are taxi ranks in the centre of all towns; some areas have radio cabs.

Telephoning

Calls may be made from card or coin operated kiosks, or from metered phones in post offices, reception lobbies, and some bars and restaurants.

"Crediphone" cards of 50 or 120 units can be bought at post offices, and shops and cafes displaying the "crediphone" sign.

LOCAL and REGIONAL calls - The Algarve is divided into three exchange areas.
* When phoning a number within your area, leave out the area code; dial only the subscriber's number.
* When phoning a number outside your area, first dial the appropriate area code, then the subscriber's number.

Algarve area codes:
089 - Faro area, including Albufeira, Almancil, Boliqueime, Loulé, Olhão, Quarteira, São Brás de Alportel, Vilamoura.
082 - Portimão area, including Alvor, Aljezur, Armação de Pera, Carvoeiro, Silves, Lagos, Monchique, Praia da Luz and Sagres.

081 - Tavira area, including Monte Gordo, Vila Nova de Cacela and Vila Real de Santo António.

NATIONAL calls - The area code for Lisbon is 01, Oporto 02. The codes for all other areas in Portugal are given on page XI at the front of the Algarve phone directory.

INTERNATIONAL calls - You can get through to most countries directly by dialling the international and national codes followed by the area code and the subscriber's number.

International and national codes:

Australia	0061	Netherlands	0031
Austria	0043	New Zealand	0064
Belgium	0032	Norway	0047
Canada	0071	South Africa	0027
Denmark	0045	Spain	0034
France	0033	Sweden	0046
Germany	0049	Switzerland	0041
Gibraltar	00350	U.K.	0044
Hongkong	00852	United States	0071
Ireland	00358	Zimbabwe	097263

* Overseas national and area codes are listed at the front of the Algarve phone directory on pages XIII to XIX
* If the overseas area code begins with 0, leave out the 0 when dialling. For example, the area code for Central London is 071, but when phoning Central London dial 004471 not 0044071.

INQUIRIES
* Overseas operators speak English, but some national operators do not.
* Inquiries about numbers in the Algarve - dial 118; elsewhere in Portugal - 090; elsewhere in Europe - 099; outside Europe - dial 098.

PHONE DIRECTORY

The Algarve phone directory is a confusing book for most visitors. A few tips in finding your way around it:
* To find the number of a subscriber in the Algarve, first determine which of the three exchange areas it is in - Faro, Portimão or Tavira.
* The exchange areas appear in the directory alphabetically. The Faro area is on pages 26 to 196; Portimão area pages 197 to 322; Tavira area pages 323 to 355.
* Each of the three exchange sections of the directory start with the area's main town, ie Faro, Portimão, Tavira, The smaller towns and villages within each exchange area follow the main town in alphabetical order.
* Even though they are in Portuguese, you might find use for the yellow pages at the back.

Tourist information offices:

AIRPORT
Faro
Tel. (089) 818582

ALBUFEIRA
Rua 5 de Outubro
Tel. (089) 512144

ALCOUTIM
Praça da República
Tel. (089) 46179

ALJEZUR
Largo do Mercado
Tel. (082) 98229

ARMAÇÃO DE PERA
Avenida Marginal
Tel. (082) 312145

CARVOEIRO
Largo da Praia
Tel. (082) 357728

CASTRO MARIM
Praça 1º do Maio
Tel. (081) 531232

FARO
Rua da Misericórdia
Tel. (089) 803604

LAGOS
Largo Marques de Pombal
Tel. (082) 763031

LOULÉ
Edifício do Castelo
Tel. (089) 63900

MONTE GORDO
Avenida Marginal
Tel. (081) 44495

OLHÃO
Largo do Lago
Tel. (089) 713936

PORTIMÃO
Largo 1º de Dezembro
Tel. (082) 23695

PRAIA DA ROCHA
Av. Tomás Cabreira
Tel. (082) 22290

QUARTEIRA
Avenida Infante Sagres
Tel. (089) 312217

SAGRES
Fortaleza
(082) 64125

SÃO BRÁS DE ALPORTEL
Rua Dr Evaristo Gago
Tel. (089) 842211

SILVES
Rua 25 de Abril
Tel. (082) 442255

TAVIRA
Praça da República
Tel. (081) 22511

VILA REAL
Outside ferry quay
Tel. (081) 43272

Head office: Rua Ataide de Oliveira, 100, Faro.
Tel. (089) 803667.

Trains

The **regional** railway line runs from Vila Real de Santo António in the east to Lagos in the west with 47 stations in between. Depending on where you are going to, it can be a good way to travel. The track runs through interesting countryside rather than hugging the coast and it gives a different perspective to the one road users see.

There are several trains daily in either direction. Most of them stop at nearly all stations. These must be avoided at all costs if you are going a long way. Peruse the timetables for the express trains.

The station (*estação*) at Vila Real de Santo António is next to the ferry. Those at Tavira, Faro, Portimão and Lagos are fairly close to the town centres. Others are not so close. Albufeira station, for example, is at Ferreiras, 6 kms from Albufeira.

Lisbon trains link with the Algarve regional line at Tunes junction near Albufeira station. The Lisbon terminus is at Barreiro on the other side of the river from Lisbon. The train fare includes a ferry-boat ride to near the city centre. Tunes - Barreiro express trains take 3 hours or less.

Timetables are available from stations, tourist information office, reception desks and travel agents.

Walking

Huge areas of the Algarve are unfenced and ideal for everyone from serious ramblers to those who just like a peaceful stroll in the countryside or along the coast. All you need is a pair of comfortable trainers or walking shoes. Very few places call for hiking boots, but flip-flops or sandals are hopeless for walking through stony or thorny countryside and positively dangerous on clifftops.

There are no rambling clubs as such, but the Liga para a Proteção da Natureza, an environmentalist group, get together for a walk on the first Saturday of every month. Visitors are welcome to join these outings which always start at 9.30am from Station Square in Portimão. For details, phone Jill Lloyd on (082) 789359 or 789663.

The regional tourist board has published a handy booklet on suggested walks. It is called *Guide to Walks in the Algarve.* Otherwise you are on your own. Go exploring. Within the bounds of common sense and common courtesy, do not worry too much about trespassing on farm or forestry land if there are no *privado* signs or fences obviously designed to keep people out.

There are countless paths and tracks, particularly in the hills and foothills, which will give enjoyment to walkers at any time of the year, though none more so than from February to June.

Water-skiing

Sheltered water, ideal for skiing, is to be found in the lagoons between Faro and Vila Real de Santo António in the eastern Algarve, and within the breakwaters at Ferragudo near Portimão at the mouth of the Arade river.

The least wind and flattest water is usually in the mornings. Lessons can be arranged, and boats and equipment can be hired at hourly rates on a number of beaches during the summer months.

Jet-skis are also available for hire on some beaches.

Windsurfing

Much of the Algarve south coast is excellent for windsurfing, but the turquoise and translucent sea here can be beguiling. Remember, it's the Atlantic and therefore powerful and sometimes erratic. And the water is often cold. Outside of high summer you may need a wet-suit. Boards and sails can be hired from any number of beaches, but it is advisable to hire only from centres which have fast boats standing by just in case windsurfers get into difficulty.

The sheltered stretches of water in the lagoons between Faro and Vila Real de Santo António, within the breakwaters at Ferragudo at the mouth of the river Arade, and off Martinhal beach just east of Sagres are all good places.

The best conditions for experienced windsurfers are when the sea is calm and there is a steady wind blowing at up to force 5 from the west. Such conditions are most likely to be encountered in the afternoons. Beginners will find conditions more to their liking in the mornings in summer when the sea is often flat and light breezes waft in from the south.

Words and expressions: English - Portuguese

On a short visit to the Algarve, you will probably be able to get by without speaking a word of Portuguese. It is a good idea, though, to learn a few everyday greetings and courteous expressions and to keep a list of other useful words and phrases handy for reference or in case you need help. In the following lists, the Portuguese is in italics with approximate pronounciations in the third column.

GREETINGS

Hello	*Olá*	ohlah
Good morning	*Bom dia*	bawn deeah
Good afternoon	*boa tarde*	boa tard
Good evening/night	*boa noite*	boa noyt
How are you?	*Como está?*	kawmoo esh**tah**
I am pleased to meet you	*Um prazer*	um pra**zair**
Goodbye	*adeus*	ahdayoosh
See you later	*até logo*	ahtay lawgoo

COURTESY

Please	*Faz favor*	fahsh favawre
Thank you (woman speaking)	*Obrigada*	obree**gah**dah
Thank you (man speaking)	*Obrigado*	obree**gah**doo
I am sorry (apologising)	*Desculpe*	desh**koo**lpe
Excuse me (when obstructing)	*Com licença*	cawn leesensah
It doesn't matter	*não faz mal*	naw fahsh mahl

NUMERALS

a quarter	*um quarto*	oom quartoo	17	*dezasete*	dezasete
half	*meio*	mayoo	18	*dezoito*	dezaoytoo
0	*zero*	zairoo	19	*dezanove*	dezanove
1	*um or uma*	oom or oomah	20	*vinte*	veengte
2	*dois or duas*	doysh or dooash	21	*vinte e um*	veengte ee oong
3	*três*	traysh	30	*trinta*	treengta
4	*quatro*	kooatroo	40	*quarenta*	kooarehngta
5	*cinco*	**seen**koo	50	*cinquenta*	seengkooehngta
6	*seis*	saysh	60	*sessenta*	sesehngt
7	*sete*	set	70	*setenta*	stehngta
8	*oito*	**oy**too	80	*oitenta*	oytehngta
9	*nove*	nawve	90	*noventa*	noovehngta
10	*dez*	desh	100	*cem*	sayng
11	*onze*	awnz	101	*cento e um*	senhgtoo ee oong
12	*doze*	dawz	110	*cento e dez*	senhgtoo ee desh
13	*treze*	trez	200	*duzentos*	doozenhgtoos
14	*catorze*	katawrze	500	*quinhentos*	keenyenhgtoosh
15	*quinze*	keengze	1000	*mil*	meal
16	*dezasseis*	dezasaysh	2000	*dois mil*	doyshmeal

DAYS OF THE WEEK

Sunday	*Domingo*
Monday	*Segunda-feira*
Tuesday	*Terça-feira*
Wednesday	*Quarta-feira*
Thursday	*Quinta-feira*
Friday	*Sexta-feira*
Saturday	*Sábado*
every day	*todos dos dias*
today	*hoje*
tomorrow	*amanhã*
this week	*esta semana*
next week	*próxima semana*

MONTHS OF THE YEAR

January	*Janeiro*
February	*Fevereiro*
March	*Março*
April	*Abril*
May	*Maio*
June	*Junho*
July	*Julho*
August	*Agosto*
September	*Setembro*
October	*Outubro*
November	*Novembro*
December	*Dezembro*

TIME

10.0am *dez horas da manhã.*   1.0pm *uma hora da tarde.*

SIGNS: bar-restaurant

Saída	Exit
Casas de banho	Toilets
Homens	Men's toilet
Senhoras	Ladies' toilet
Proibido (Não) fumar	No smoking
Pronto pagamento	Pay as you order

SIGNS: filling station

Ar	Air
Lavagem automática	Car wash
Gasóleo	Deisel fuel
Mistura	Motorbike two-stroke
Óleo	Oil
Gasolina super	Petrol - leaded super
Gasolina sem chumbo	- unleaded super
Gasolina normal	- normal
Pneus	Tyres
Água	Water - normal
Água distilada	- distilled

SIGNS: on the road

Atenção	Caution
Cuidado	Caution
Desvio	Diversion
Espere	Wait
Estacionamento proibido	No parking
Obras na estrada	Road works
Parque de estacionamento	Car park
Passagem proibida	No entry
Perigo	Danger

POST OFFICE TERMS

correio azul	**koorrayoo azool**	express post
marco postal	**mark**oo postal	post box
bilhete postal	beeyet post**al**	postcard
correio	**koorrayoo**	post office
registada	regeeshtada	registed
selo	**seloo**	stamp
telefone	telefone	telephone

COMMON QUESTIONS

Do you have...?	*Tem...?*	teng
Do you speak English?	*Fala inglês?*	falah eenglesh
How far is...?	*Que distância...?*	ke distanseeah
How long does it take...?	*Quanto tempo leva...?*	kwantoo tempoo leveh
How many Kilometres...?	*Quantos Kilometros... ?*	kwantoo killawmetrosh
How much?	*Quanto custa...?*	kwantoo cushtah
May I have the bill?	*A conta?*	ah contah
What time...?	*A que horas...?*	ah ke oarash
Where can I find...?	*Onde posso encontrar...?*	ond possoo encontrar
Where can I get...?	*Onde posso arranjar..?*	ond possoo arrangar
Where is the nearest...?	*Onde fica a mais perto...?*	ond feekah ah maish pertoo
Which way to...?	*Qual a direção para...?*	kwal ah deerehsau

PRONUNCIATION OF PLACE NAMES

Albufeira	alboo**fayra**
Alvor	**al**vor
Armação de Pera	arma**sau** de **peara**
Almancil	almanseal
Aljezur	alzhzoor
Carvoeiro	carvewhereoo
Faro	faroo
Ferreiras	fer**air**ash
Lagoa	lahgoa
Lagos	lahgosh
Loulé	lowlay
Monchique	monshiek
Olhão	olyau
Portimão	porteemau
Praia da Luz	pryah de loosh
Quarteira	quart**air**ah
Quinta do Lago	keentah dough lahgo
São Brás	sau brash
Sagres	**saag**resh
Silves	silvzh
Tavira	ta**veer**ah
Vilamoura	villamoorah
Vila Real	villa reeal

INDEX

Notes